MARTIN BRODSKY

ALLOW ME TO WASTE YOUR TIME

PETTY THIEF PRESS

Cover and book design by Nathaniel Roy
Illustrations and author photo by Kody Kohlman

The essay "Touch Me" first appeared in *Hobart*
Excerpts from "epigraph," "style," "my friend william" from *Mockingbird Wish Me Luck* by Charles Bukowski. ©1972 by Charles Bukowski. Used by permission of HarperCollins Publishers.

ISBN: 979-8-9934507-4-2

www.martinbrodsky.com
www.pettythiefpress.com

For the *we*.

ALLOW ME TO WASTE YOUR TIME

CONTENTS

A word before we begin:

The right path through life . . . we're all trying to choose it. But how to measure *right*? Money, status, power? Friends, family, relationships? Or is it simply the freedom to choose which of these actually matter? If the answer were simple, we might not have a thing called God nor influencers.

From the day we're born, our path heads straight into a tangle of desire, expectation, and circumstance. By the time we realize the choice is ours, how much of our path has already been defined by parents, friends, home-towns, and those forces of society we can't even see? This all comes, by the way, before we even get online.

These days it's fair to say the internet can't be trusted: perfect photos, witty commentary, a barrage of advertisements for new scents to make you irresistible . . . these things are half-truths at best, usually grifts for your money, your time, and your attention to boot. But when the brightest minds of our generation are shilling for the corporate technocrats, is it any surprise we buy in?

Somehow they've made the endless scroll seem like a reasonable place to find that right path (or, if nothing else, a readymade escape from the wrong one). Which leads to the real problem: distraction. Pulling us from the hard work of figuring out what we care about, what might actually make us happy, the algorithm *knows* FOMO isn't just some cute buzzword but something to be exploited for its gain and our loss.

The problem of distraction starts when we don't know what we want—fertile ground for others to make us surrogate for their own desires—so let's agree right now to keep that from happening.

As they say, if you don't stand for something you'll fall for anything. And if I'm falling down a trendy new rabbit hole every five minutes, how can I find the right path through life? My take: it comes down to believing in something with enough conviction to swat away the distraction pulling us off course.

I'm not sure I have the right path figured out—but I believe in a few things that seem to help:

DON'T BE CONVENTIONAL

Society feels like a runaway freight train, maybe now more than ever, and to be conventional is to lay down another six feet of track, with your back as the rail, for that train to keep going a little while longer. To be conventional is to ignore the motives behind the screens in our hands that want us to do their bidding. To be conventional is to believe that the right path will appear with a glowing neon sign that says RIGHT THIS WAY, without any effort at all.

You know the famous last lines of Robert Frost's *The Road Not Taken*:

> Two roads diverged in a wood, and I—
> I took the one less traveled by,
> And that has made all the difference.

Yet all of the poem before this is about figuring out which path to take. Why is it easier to celebrate the glorified destination, ignoring the journey required to make it there? The answer is convention. Convention creates a well-trodden path for our feet to mindlessly follow, freeing our eyes to search the horizon, awash in the illusion of choice.

I'm not saying we ought to throw out convention wholesale, just that we should see it for what it is. That we must deliberately choose the conventional pieces of life we want and actively discard the rest. What you and I decide to keep will be different. And that's the beauty of it! Convention asks us to homogenize, blending our individual colors until they're indecipherable from one another, but we need all the colors to shine. So let them fly. Celebrating someone else's differences might be the most unconventional thing a person could do.

When we question convention in pursuit of another path, a better path, one less traveled by, the powers that be sow doubt in our minds. And on our own, as individuals, we'd never make it through. We need each other. We need those who believe in another way. To escape convention, we need to find our people.

FIND YOUR PEOPLE

Let's stick with the digital. If you go back to Facebook in the very beginning, it was actually a tool for people to connect: stay in touch with friends, find long-lost acquaintances, maybe even meet someone new. It feels innocent to imagine the place without the newsfeed, the division, let alone the algorithm. The original intent of social media—real connection—tapped into a human desire that cannot be buried beneath even the headiest stream of viral video content.

When people connect, big things happen. Social progress, evolution, revolution. People have the means to organize, evading censorship and control like never before. And to think banning TikTok is only about foreign security concerns? Right. If only you ignore what's also happening from within.

That's the big picture, yet I think it's even more interesting to look at this on a smaller, human-to-human scale. Journalists no longer need newspapers to publish their reportage, they go direct to readers on Substack. Filmmakers put their work on YouTube and Vimeo. Artists, thinkers, organizers, and agents of change from all sectors can bypass the regulatory forces of the government, of the corporations, of conventional society and speak directly to their people. The cultural gatekeepers—legacy media, Hollywood, traditional publishers—remain at their posts, but the masses are outside and already scaling the fence.

If all these alternatives abound, then why are we still here wondering about how to find the right path?

Because a constant diet of rapid-fire content slaps plaque onto our neural pathways. We won't survive for long with distraction shunting blood from our brains. As far as I can tell, the only solution is to slow down.

SLOW DOWN

Life isn't about the new new new! That's some bullshit concocted by profiteers to keep us glued to the screen with our fingers gripped on the credit card. Speed is their ally. The antidote is slowing down, cultivating life with patience. One way to do this is by appreciating art.

There's nothing better than when a piece of art lingers in your head. Read poetry. Read it again. Revisit old posts, old videos, old stories. Sometimes when you go back the effect is completely different. When you return to a piece of art, you *feel* how far you've come. This is about personal growth. I first watched Sean Penn's adaptation of Jon Krakauer's *Into the Wild* when I was in college. Inspired, I went and free-soloed a cliff outside of town; ten years later I saw it again and thought, what a foolish kid: regarding both Chris McCandless and myself.

What is art but a mirror? A reflection of who we are in that very moment. Maybe a better analogy is a prism: art takes whatever light we're shining from within and beams it back to us, revealing the true colors inside. Isn't this why we seek out music to suit our mood? (I certainly didn't listen to metal in seventh grade because I was happy.) Sometimes art shakes things loose that we didn't even know were in there, revealing new parts of ourselves—parts that might pull us out of the rut and onto new paths—and this cannot happen in the time it takes to flick your thumb across the screen. So take your time with art, with life, let this settle in.

I learned the word *philistine* the other day, referring to a person who is hostile to the arts, to culture, to a life of the mind. I also learned that 46% of Americans read *zero* books last year. A friend of mine was recently at a book convention and overheard a couple of joes at the hotel bar. "I haven't read a book since like high school," one of them bragged. As William S. Burroughs once suggested, intellectuals are considered deviant in the United States of America.

If you've come this far, I'm guessing being a deviant doesn't bother you. To find the right path through life, you've got to think; to think, you've got to question convention; to question convention, you need to find your people; and to find your people, you need to slow down. But all of that simply requires paying attention. And that's what we're trying to do here.

Alright. Let's get to it.

M.B.
2025

DON'T BE CONVENTIONAL

FIGURING THINGS OUT
A STORY ABOUT IMPROVISATION

Nobody knows what they're doing. And I've come to believe that anybody who says they do is full of shit.

Sure, we might have a few things figured out: a job, a house, a relationship (to use some old standby milestones), but these achievements are tenuous, always requiring more work, more attention, more evolution. So the figuring continues . . . on and on, forever.

We create plans, set ourselves goals, develop methods for achieving them, all of this to make sense of what's going on around us. Yet they only get us so far. As the saying goes, the best laid plans of mice and men often go awry. Or to quote the infamous Mike Tyson: "Everybody has plans until they get hit for the first time."

A breakup, a layoff, doors unexpectedly closing, these are life's punches. And when our plans fall apart, what are we left with to find our way?

One tool: improvisation.

When I was kid, my grandmother signed me up for a ceramics class. As we pounded clay, the teacher told us—insisted, even—that there are no mistakes in art. Being young elementary students, praised elsewhere in first grade by Mrs. Walker for writing neatly and coloring within the lines, this was some subversive shit.

Some kids didn't believe it. They had to know if they were right or wrong. The idea of any grey area haywired their black-and-white view of the world. And to a large extent this grey area continues to short-circuit many adult brains, too.

But you can't figure out anything in that state of mind. When plans go awry, those black-and-white fantasies disappear. You have no choice but to muddle through the grey. So instead of waiting on some User Manual for Life, you've got to put that trust in yourself.

Enter improvisation.

Improvisation, by definition, requires bushwhacking into the unknown. Be it sailing off the edge of the map, or launching into the chord changes of Coltrane's *Giant Steps*. It takes confidence to go for it, but we're a lot more capable than we give ourselves credit for. And what exactly is confidence in this regard?

Let's take the idea of jazz musician Bobby McFerrin that improvisation is simply the courage to keep going.

Courage is a daunting word, evoking epic images of charging into battle, scaling mountains, making impossible decisions. But in its essence, courage is much simpler than that . . . it consists of one word: *yes*.

As it happens, the number one rule of improv theater is to say *yes*. When an actor makes a move, throws out a line, you must go with it. And then you must take those ideas and make them your own, always maintaining forward momentum. Nothing kills momentum like the word *no*.

This reminds me of an article I once tore out of Surfer Magazine a long time ago, which I carried in my wallet for years. It was called "Advice for Travelling Solo." Top of the list: say yes to every opportunity that comes your way.

Now, I understand quite well the need to protect your time, that saying *yes* always means saying *no* to something else. Yet the opposite seems equally important: the best way to say *no* is by saying *yes* to something else. It's about being deliberate. Dizzy Gillespie, yet another jazz legend—they knew a lot about improvisation—famously reflected: "It's taken me all my life to learn what not to play."

In other words, don't be arbitrary with your *no*.

This extends even to things we consider fun, like vacation. My newest motto is no shitty vacations. You have to pay for them on the back end, catching up on work no matter what, so you'd better make them count. And this remains relevant to all of life. If I value my time, I cut out needles meetings. If I value my relationships, I cut out toxic friends. If I want to write, I cut out the activities I don't actually care about.

But I digress. To bring it back home, *yes* requires courage, courage enables improvisation, and improvisation leads to *yes*. It's a practice, I suppose, which never ends. Crafting a life takes time, or like my father says at sixty-two: I'm still a work in progress.

A work in progress, of course, means still figuring things out. Sometimes in life we get it right. Sometimes we don't.

But there are no mistakes in art.

AGING OUT
A STORY ABOUT YOUTH

A few years ago, as he approached ninety, I asked my grandfather how old he felt. Without hesitation, he said: "Same as I did in high school." This is a man married for sixty-five years with children, grandchildren, great-grandchildren, not to mention countless tales of (mis)adventure traveling the world for both business and pleasure—and, yet, he still feels eighteen.

The suffragette Gertrude Nelson Andrews once wrote: "A man at eighty should be a masterpiece."

I think my grandfather has done well to carve and polish his life into something worth admiring, if less celebrated than a Michelangelo. But the art in the way he's lived has not been lost on his friends and family. He'd be the first to tell you that's all that matters in the end, anyway.

With my thirty-seventh birthday on the horizon, I can't help but contrast the mandate to live a beautiful life with the old adage that many people die at twenty-five and aren't buried until they are seventy five. That about sums up the two available paths for us.

Now, I like to believe I've got plenty of time to work on the masterpiece while dodging both the literal and figurative mortician, but the thing is age creeps up on you fast. One day you're driving around with your buddies on a high-school Friday night, looking for anything to do; next thing you know, your hair is thinning, hangovers last for three days, and there are all these fucking bills to pay.

Reconciling the reality of getting older with the imposter syndrome that so often accompanies it, I sometimes look in the mirror and wonder who the hell is staring back at me: this rather domestic, married father of two who's held down one job for the better part of a decade—the same person, that is, who rented a dozen different apartments and worked seasonal jobs the decade before that so as not be "tied down."

I look back on those times of utter freedom with nostalgia, considering the responsibilities I shoulder now, but the ironic thing is that I also remember yearning to settle down amidst the aimlessness of that time. Which is to say, I'm not convinced you can ever be all-in on one lifestyle—there are just too many possibilities, alternative realities that might just become *reality*—and, often enough, the change seems to happen without you even realizing it. So what to do?

My late grandmother, the one married to my grandfather for those sixty-five years, always said: life is not a dress rehearsal. It's sort of become a family motto. There are a lot of clichés about living in the present and making the most of life, but I like the dress rehearsal one because it puts us in as the actors of our own lives. And just as a good stage actor gains experience—the performance becoming more comfortable, more natural, more provocative—so goes navigating the trials and tribulations of life.

I also like the actor analogy because it allows you to put on the costume of whatever age suits the occasion. Business meeting: forty-five. Taking the kids to the zoo: twelve. Going on a date with your wife: twenty-six. And, ultimately, there's that ever-present age you feel in your head.

For as long as I can remember, my grandfather claimed to be 39 (eighteen must've been a little too far-fetched). It was always funny, especially when my parents surpassed that. But as one of the liveliest people I know, I have no doubt there's something to it.

Seems like young at heart actually starts in the head.

SEARCHING FOR SIMPLICITY
A STORY ABOUT RETURNING

Simplicity is not hard to find. After all, we're born with it. Eat, sleep, poop—doesn't get much simpler than that. The problem is how to hold onto that simplicity?

Of course, life inevitably gets in the way. Before we know it, we're caught in a complex web of responsibility that is anything but simple. But not all is lost, for there is another kind of simplicity out there waiting for us ... the simplicity on the other side of complexity.

The poet and physician Oliver Wendell Holmes Sr. once wrote: "I would not give a fig for the simplicity on this side of complexity, but I would give my life for the simplicity on the other side of complexity." Whereas we're all granted simplicity at birth, the entry prize for being human, simplicity on the other side of complexity must be realized, learned and earned. And not everyone gets over the hump.

So what is this other kind of simplicity? And how do we find it?

Let's start with a fable about Picasso ...

A woman recognizes the old artist sketching in the park. "It's you—Picasso, the great artist! Oh, you must sketch my portrait!" she insists. After studying her for a moment, he uses a single pencil stroke to create her portrait. "Incredible!" the woman gushes. "You captured my very essence. How much do I owe you?" Picasso replies, "Five thousand francs, madam." The woman is outraged. "How could you want so much money for this picture? It only took you a second to draw it!" Picasso smiles. "No, madam, it took my whole life."

What is simpler than a line? But when Picasso draws a line it's more than merely ink on paper. It's a lifetime of paying attention distilled into a single act.

The writer Anaïs Nin once observed: "We don't see things as they are; we see them as we are." As a homebuilder, I walk through a house and see details a layperson wouldn't. A doctor looks at the body and sees an array of systems working in perfect synchronization. A painter sees the world in colors and forms.

This noticing takes time. Yet there's an inverse relationship between the results of such noticing and the amount of time spent acquiring the skill. An experienced plumber can fix a pipe in less time than a novice plumber; same with a skilled surgeon replacing a knee; or an artist sketching a portrait. This is part of the simplicity, the ease with which we accomplish the things we set out to do.

Getting to the simplicity on the other side of complexity takes time. You cannot cheat your way through time. This is why we all must start as apprentices before becoming masters, and students before teachers.

However, I worry that we as a society *are* trying to cheat by engineering a path over the hump of complexity. Nothing exemplifies this more than AI. It seems pretty clear that the jobs AI is best suited to overtake are the entry-level positions: junior copywriter, junior programmer, all the things we do early on. If these aren't available, how will anyone become skilled enough in a given field to push it into new territory? Or creatively solve problems without relying on the technology itself? Wouldn't that be a planned obsolescence of our own kind?

From a humanist standpoint what I fear most is a collective helplessness of the average person, derived from AI kneecapping one's ability to even get off the ground. In other words, AI might not be so much a nuclear explosion that wipes out humanity, but rather a societal failure to launch.

Because the "launch" is what pushes us over the hump of complexity toward simplicity on the other side. It's us being able to find a purpose and act on it. It's our being able to close what Ira Glass calls the "Taste Gap." Or the idea that when we start out our ambition is driven by our own good taste, though our abilities can't yet match it. That disconnect can last for years and it derails people. But keep going! Only persistence will close the gap to make the art and life you want.

The ability to make what we find tasteful, to live a life that feels truly ours, this is the mark of simplicity. Which is not to say easy. It takes a lot of sustained effort to get to the other side. For inspiration, let's enjoy the work of a few people who've made it.

First, listen to Philip Glass' masterpiece written for the Dalai Lama, *Mad Rush*. Read Raymond Carver's sparse and lasting prose. Then look at the evolution of Piet Mondrian's painting from early in his career to the end.

Some might label all of this work minimalist, but I think it's more about a human knowing *exactly* what they want to say and stripping that down to its absolute essence, honed over a lifetime of pursuit.

In many ways, there's a certain playfulness to these artworks. The simplicity in them evokes the Buddhist idea of the Beginner's Mind: maintaining the curiosity and eagerness of a beginner, no matter how advanced your expertise. This is similar to a saying chess players use: a move only a beginner—or a grandmaster—would play.

In this regard, perhaps the path to simplicity on the other side of complexity looks less like a bell-curve hump and more like a circle.

For the best example, I'll return to my grandfather who has certainly discovered this more profound form of simplicity, the superfluous pieces of his life left behind years ago. When we get together as a family, you know who he seems to have the most in common with? The children, just like a perfect circle.

I guess sometimes it's as simple as that.

SOCIETAL CROSS SECTIONS
A STORY ABOUT STEREOTYPES

For the past ten years I've been making a living as a custom homebuilder. Having worked in a cubicle before that, the joys of using my hands and being outside are high on the list, but my favorite part of the job has to do with the people I see every day. As a project manager, the gig cuts a cross-section through society—meaning I talk to everyone from ditch diggers to millionaire financiers, architects graduated from Harvard and tradesmen emigrated from Mexico / Russia / Ukraine / Honduras. There's no telling who might show up on a given day. The only thing certain is that none of these conversations sound anything alike. It's "fucking this" and "fucking that" with the electrician; "the more cost-effective approach here would be. . ." with the homeowner; geeking out on tile patterns with the interior designers; and swapping dirty euphemisms across the language barrier with the guys.

Some might say it's disingenuous to shift your words around in this way, but I think it's like changing shoes. You don't wear hiking boots to a nice dinner; you don't wear tassel loafers on the trail. Because you've got to fit within the scene around you—at least that's the goal. (Enter the proverbial loud American ordering *grand expressos* in some European café, gaining stares from everyone . . . read the room, man.)

On a daily basis, though, diversity can be hard to come by. Similar to, say, custom jewelers or loan sharks, few vocations see a wide swath of society. Some exceptions: gas station attendants, stadium ticket takers, pharmacists. Because, for the most part, we find our people and get comfortable. Then when it comes to the unfamiliar, we pretty much only have the blunt tool of stereotype to work with. I guess that's human nature. However, it would be a mistake to pigeon-hole any portion of society, let alone an individual, upon such corrupted ideas wholesale. We all know the "exceptions" who "aren't like that"—you know, friends who don't fit the given stereotype. Of course, most people qualify when you actually talk to them.

And this is when it gets interesting, because people breaking free of stereotypes is the greatest act of cultural subversion one could make. As Charles Bukowski, the scum-dredging beauty-divining poet of Los Angeles, once wrote:

> *the world is full of shipping clerks*
> *who have read*
> *the Harvard Classics.*

I'll personally attest to that. Take this one crusty old plumber I know who loves opera, holding a regular *musik nacht* where a group of toilet sales reps and pipe runners get together to discuss Wagner and Verdi and Puccini like they're buddies.

Or take the carpenters who listen to Alan Watts' lectures while ripping down plywood, subsequently discussing their weekend Harley rides through the lens of eastern philosophy—*Zen and the Art of Motorcycle Maintenance* in the flesh.

When you see guys like this rolling around town in their pickup trucks, who would guess? Yet the more I see it happen, the more I think this truth stays secret because it's fun to know the truth when others don't, to make connections where others won't.

However, in the end, the only stereotypes you can really break are those that apply to yourself. So I'll wrap this one up with a story of my own:

It was my toddler's last music class and I'd yet to see what this was all about. So after laying out the framers on a stud wall, I drove to the studio, untied my work boots, and placed them next to the row of tiny shoes. I sat down beside my wife and child, crossed my legs and started clapping along to the teacher's jangling guitar. And then we sang, "hello everybody, we're so glad to see you."

Indeed.

BEING WEIRD IS NORMAL (NORMAL PEOPLE ARE WEIRD)

A STORY ABOUT FITTING IN

Fitting in is overrated. But for a while in my life, it seemed like the only way to survive.

Now, I don't regret the years I tried to be normal—you've got to learn the rules before you break them, after all—but why did I care so much about being just like everyone else?

It didn't start out that way. In kindergarten I remained an unreconstructed *weirdo*: cracking open acorns on the playground, pretending the insides were cheese, eating them. Little kids are gloriously weird. In fact, I think we're all born our own weird selves and we stay that way until something profound happens: friends.

School teaches us more than reading, writing, and arithmetic. You soon learn that some people are cool and some people are not. The criteria for the designation might be mysterious, but the end result cuts black and white. God bless the people who don't let this bother them—I cannot claim that for myself.

For me, school was like joining a flock of birds. Whenever the group moved this way or that, I went along with it, if only because the next closest kid did the same thing. What else do you expect when you and everyone else (even those who fake it) have no idea where they're going? Because the last thing you want is to stray too far and get picked off.

In other words: Being normal is a disappearing act. Wearing the shoes, the shirt, the haircut, saying the right things—fitting in perfectly—disappearing is the point, right?

I don't know if this is true for everyone, but the times I've tried to fit in most line up perfectly with the times I've felt least secure about who I am. And when I couldn't believe in myself, I believed in what was normal.

After sacrificing myself to being normal for years, though, life got pretty rough. Confidence was at an all-time low. But if (false) friends got me into that mess, (real) friends got me out. Friends who through all kinds of social miscues came to know me for who I really was, and didn't care that I was weird.

At some point, hopefully, you realize that normal is boring. That rewards await those willing to be different, which goes back to the rules we learn in the schoolyard, those ways we were 'supposed' to act for the sake of the group. As music producer Rick Rubin emphasizes in his book *The Creative Act*, the key is to honor your own voice—develop it, nurture it, and let it guide your choices.

Rubin has worked with some notorious weirdos and their success backs this up. Of course, what he's saying, however, doesn't only apply to music—it's a way of being.

It took a while, but eventually I got a whole lot more comfortable straying from the crowd, being different. I didn't fully understand what changed until years later, when a friend explained the process: learn to love yourself.

Learn to love yourself. That's everything, isn't it? Not everyone has gotten there in their heart of hearts—I'm still working on it myself—but in the meantime I think this starts by simply being kind to yourself.

I know one thing for sure: if you love yourself, you don't want to disappear. And if you don't want to disappear, well, you're not normal.

Here's to my fellow weirdos.

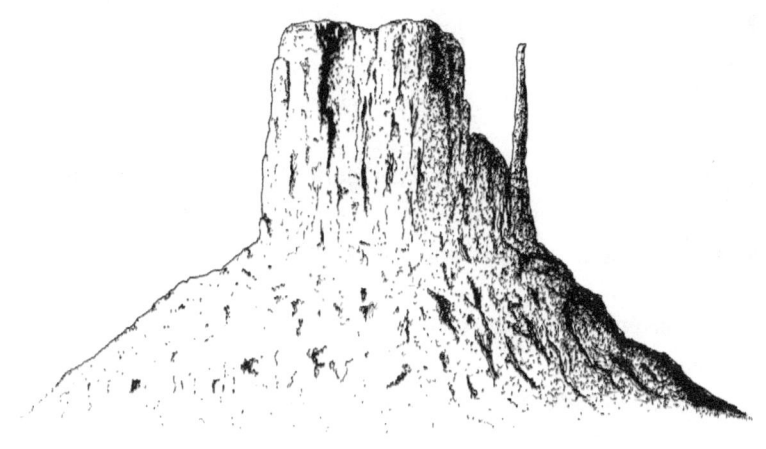

INTO THE RUST
A SHORT STORY

She liked things old because of that farmhouse.

Where she grew up barefoot on creaking floors, playing in the lace draperies with her barn cats, lying at night in her four-post bed listening to conversations drift through the transom above the door . . . sometimes conversations she wasn't supposed to hear.

And so, when it came time to leave, the shine of the city held no luster in her eyes. She pushed away the highrise job her wits could have landed, bought a 1987 Volkswagon camper van and pointed its snub nose west. Taking off for those vast and open spaces in pursuit of something more ruthless: her past.

With dust in the air, bouncing down the old highway, listening to the groan of the coil springs beneath her van, she drove deep into the desert toward the edge of the reservation.

She had discovered her Navajo blood after her mother had stuffed a DNA test in her Christmas stocking and desperately wondered what love had put those drops into her Scotch-Irish line.

Signs of it had been bleached by generations like bones in the sun. But the question—that vacant, tearing silence of her ancestors—burned in her like a rising juniper ember, flickering orange against the night.

Sagebrush musk rolled through her windows and the red sandstone towers rose proud and stoic into the valley of monuments, like ancient elders holding space in the round and turquoise sky.

A deserted roadside stall appeared in the heat. She stopped and read the faded sign: cold drinks, fry bread, jewelry, native crafts. A frayed American flag wrapped itself lazily around the pole. She stepped under the tin roof, thick with patina from winter storms and summer suns.

The long empty table creaked under her weight as she leaned against it, staring at the stone towers miles away. The wind whispered through the empty stall, playing with the tips of her hair, drifting out unchanged . . . like a conversation she wasn't supposed to hear.

CULTIVATING A VIBE
A STORY ABOUT COLLECTION

You might divide everything in life into two categories: utility and beauty. These aren't mutually exclusive, of course. Nearly anything could be both: a shirt, a building, a relationship. But in this increasingly pragmatic world, why does beauty matter? What do we lose if the focus is merely on functionality? Let's get into this: what does beauty really mean for us as individuals, for the world all around? How do we recognize it, cultivate it, attract it?

To clear the air, looks have nothing to do with it. Beauty derives from an unseeable place, but not unknowable. We're used to taking in the world in visually, but since beauty rises from the depths we have to abandon our eyes . . . and feel it.

Enter, the vibe.

Everything around us is literally vibrating. That's why you feel a difference when sitting in an IKEA chair versus something handcrafted. You may be saying, well, a chair is a chair—but even in the most strictly utilitarian worldview, the quality is different. And though you may justify this through modes of mass production, attention to detail, etc. etc., the difference is actually in the consciousness behind it.

Some would say this consciousness inhabits everything, regardless of sentience. Alan Watts used to ring a bell during his lectures, explaining that even *this* is a rudimentary form of consciousness. What is real consciousness but understanding the reason behind something, its intention, its purpose?

The purpose of a bell is to ring. Simple enough. The purpose of a human, though, is a hell of a lot more complex. Which is why when it comes to meeting people, sometimes you feel their vibe and sometimes you don't.

An old friend describes it like this: every one of us operates on our own wavelength. When we meet each other these wavelengths interact, either amplifying or diminishing one another. In the worst cases, the wavelengths cancel each other out, flatlining completely. I'm sure we've all tried to force these kinds of relationships—but forget it, move on, there's nothing there. On occasion, however, these wavelengths coalesce and amplify and within a few minutes it might feel like you've known each other forever. (Who knows, maybe you have?)

This is hard science, not some woo woo bullshit. Graph out a vibration and what do you get . . . a wavelength. And if you accept that, then what is our life but a plotted collection of every vibration we've surrounded ourselves with?

Our own vibe comes from deep in the lifeforce—you might call that our personality—but it's soon shaped by every person in our life; not only every person, but every*thing*. Each item added to and subtracted from the mix affects it. The complexity is vast. Cultivating a vibe means curating the collection of relationships, experiences and objects around you, continuously choosing which to keep in the milieu and which to discard.

I say the more things in your collection the better. Meet more people, read more books, surround yourself with *more* as to craft your vibe into exactly who you want to be. There's resiliency in such maximalism, a system reinforced by not putting too much stock into any one aspect. It creates a healthy ecosystem: if you decide to remove something from the mix, the other vibes repair the rift; and if you add something, it won't overshadow all the rest.

In this way you can try things, experiment, explore, without fear of any misstep having too great an impact. So liberate yourself in a diverse collection of vibes. Don't succumb to the dangers of minimalism. Perhaps there is a life-changing magic to tidying up, as Marie Kondo has said, but such action ought to come with a word of caution. Taken too far, consolidation toward only the most essential veers awfully close to utilitarianism. For beauty to survive in that stark environment is a tall order, requiring a singular vibe that can stand entirely on its own.

That's not me. Nor is it most people I know. For us it's about finding beauty out there in the world, bringing home bits and pieces and adding them to the collection. Then enjoying the buzz.

MY UNCLE, THE ARTIST

A STORY ABOUT BEING COOL

One of my earliest memories of my uncle, the artist, isn't about art at all—but that he kept a Harley Davidson motorcycle in his bedroom. Why did he do that?

"Because it was *cool*," he told me. And it was cool. He *is* cool.

Having lived on his own terms long before I was born, my uncle, the artist, seems to approach life itself like he's making a piece of art. With his long pony tail, wild glasses, his uncompromisingly loud style, jewelry slung around his wrists and neck, you only have to take one look at the guy to know Scott Brandt not your typical fellow.

But being different, on its own, doesn't make a person cool.

WHAT IS COOL?

In the opening pages of *The Art Spirit*, his seminal book on the artist's life, Robert Henri writes: "When the artist is alive in any person, whatever his kind of work may be, he becomes an inventive, searching, daring, self-expressing creature. He becomes interesting to other people."

Interesting to other people: I think that's a good start as to why so many artists are cool. They have a way of drawing you in, a kind of questing personality that cannot be contained but must be expressed, which in turn expresses something in us, the audience. In other words, artists have this innate ability to take an idea and pursue it, and perhaps we can't help but live vicariously through them.

Yet this speaks to a thing artists have when it might actually be something they don't have which draws us in. In a word, artists seem *free*. And what might they be free from? Convention.

My uncle would be the first to admit—and celebrate—that he has not led a conventional life. It took him a long time to settle down and even then a restless spirit kept him travelling the world, seeing new places, meeting new people, bringing back fresh fodder for his work.

Being cool is unconventional, by definition, and artists are unconventional people. It stands to reason that, since *unconventional* and *conventional* are mutually exclusive, the cooler you are the less conventional you are.

But a cool life isn't an easy life. Giving up convention means giving up convenience—the two words share their Latin roots—and in this modern world where convenience is synonymous with ease, the cool person gives up the easy life exactly *because* they are cool.

It's not convenient to be cool, nor is it cool to be convenient. And in this way, coolness and success, in the traditionally American sense (picket fence and all that), have a strange relationship.

(UN)CONVENTIONALITY

In 1983, at twenty-three years old, my uncle took a job at an interior design firm but got fired after the receptionist left the boss to date him. After that, he enrolled in art school and hasn't worked for anyone else since. Though uncompromising in his art, he also recognized the hard truth of making ends meet. As he said:

"As a visual artist, putting out what you want without caring what others think doesn't always mean it will be sellable. If you can't make a living selling what you produce, then you'll have to take a job doing what you would rather not. Or you live a lifestyle whereby you become your own boss."

My uncle has always loved classic and exotic cars and motorcycles (see the opening paragraph). So he built a successful business selling them. In addition to making art, he's been doing this for 40 years, building himself a comfortable life in the process.

The starving artist cliché exists for a reason; but there's nothing inherently cool about destitution, just as there's nothing inherently uncool about success. In the end, they exist in tension against one another.

This tension is a cultural phenomenon and the best question might be: wouldn't both art and money be better off, if our culture cared more about creativity?

BUILDING A CULTURE TO SUPPORT COOL

In the 90s my uncle lived in both Paris and Florence.

"Both thriving cities for the arts," he said. "Both forward-thinking cities that allowed artists to express themselves fully, and gravitational in the art world for at least the last 1,500 years. If it weren't for the Medici family, the Renaissance and the world as we know it would be a very different place. They welcomed free thinkers and opposing viewpoints, in order to excel in almost every field. They were also very accepting of people. Let's face it, both Leonardo and Michelangelo were gay in a time where anywhere else in the world they would have been condemned, jailed and killed. Yet, in Florence they were allowed to shine like a beacon in spite of their sexual preference, which had nothing to do with their abilities."

The Medici family made their fortune in banking, but were more importantly great patrons of the arts, financing among many others: Leonardo,
Michelangelo, Donatello and Raphael (yes, that's all four of the teenage
mutant ninja turtles).

Every culture goes through periods of expansion and contraction. If
you care for etymology, this is baked into the very names of our dueling
modern political philosophies of *progressivism* and *conservatism*: to progress is to expand, to conserve is to contract.

It should be no surprise that the present situation is one of contraction. Of
course, we all have to pay the bills but I wonder if the next Michelangelo is
out there driving Ubers because rent is due and no one's buying his works of
genius, so they're shoved beside the water heater in his walk-up apartment.

And where are the modern-day Medicis? The cynic in me would say no one
cares about art anymore. But I believe people *do* care about art—if anything,
they just don't realize it. I could cite statistics of record-breaking concert
attendance but I'd rather discuss a viral video of the flash mob version of
Beethoven's Ode to Joy, by the Orquestra Simfònica del Vallès, in the town
square of Sabadell, Spain.

This is hands-down my favorite thing the internet has ever produced. The
people feel it! Young and old, alike. I mean, I still feel it and I've probably
watched it fifty times. Interestingly, a bank sponsored the performance,
which some people take issue with. But in our corporatocracy, what's the
difference between Banc de Sabadell and the Medici family—they were
bankers, after all.

Perhaps the patrons will come. Or maybe we band together and crowd-
source patronage for each other. The truth is nobody is going to save our
culture except us. You and me. And ultimately, finding something you
believe in and fighting for it is the coolest thing a person can do, artist
or not.

LIFE AS ART

My uncle has always been fond of the idea that if you don't stand for something, you'll fall for anything.

We might not all identify as artists, but the thing that makes artists cool—coming up with ideas and acting on them, holding enough curiosity to question the way things are, how they could be better, more beautiful—this is within us all. And, ironically, that makes everyone an artist.

My uncle, the artist, is cool not so much because he makes art, but that he *is* art. Some people are like that. I've referenced before the suffragette Gertrude Nelson Andrews who wrote: "A man at eighty should be a masterpiece."

Well, couple that with an idea often credited to Leonardo Da Vinci himself: Art is never finished, only abandoned. And all I can say is what is life but a work of art that is never finished?

Your art is your art, even if it's only living life the best you can. But it's never too late to be cool.

EMBRACING THE LIMINAL SPACE
A STORY ABOUT TRANSITIONS

WHAT DOES IT MEAN, THOUGH?

Horror movies use a slick trick to keep people unsettled. The characters are always stuck in between places—hallways (The Shining), roads (Halloween), stairs (The Exorcist)—and you might think the bad guys make it scary, but it's actually the space itself.

Dial back the psychosis and you've got a working definition of liminal space: the in-between, the transitional stages of life, the threshold dividing *here* (our current state) from *there* (where we want to be). Generally people get uncomfortable lingering in such places, just like you wouldn't stand in the middle of the crosswalk for too long, because we want to get on with it and land on the other side. We can thank our culture for hardwiring this desire into us, yet it seems a few of those wires have come loose.

ALRIGHT KID, NOW YOU'RE AN ADULT

Traditionally, liminal space refers to cultural rites of passage. The moment in the middle: no longer a boy, not yet a man. Not long ago, most societies contained longstanding rites of passage—coming of age ceremonies, vision quests, marriage rituals—but with the broad cultural decline in these rites over the last one-hundred years, the concept of liminality has filled the void and expanded to include the most basic transitions within society—graduation, marriage, kids, divorce—things that aren't necessarily agreed upon in a culture, and may not even apply to most individuals.

There's much to lament about the downfall of traditional rites of passage, even if some were problematic in their own right. In many ways, we've been cast adrift, these social maps showing at least one clear path through life lost to shifting values and the mechanics of cultural evolution.

It's tempting to say we must go back and reestablish the rites of passage. But when a storm comes through and levels the town, you've got to clear the debris entirely before you can build it back up. So, let's finish the demolition . . . there's never been a *this* side and *that* side.

IT'S ALL TRANSITION, BABY

Imagine life is a hallway. Behind these doors we expect comfortable rooms—rooms of final destinations, rooms of goals achieved, rooms of satisfaction—but when we open the doors to these rooms, what if there are actually just more hallways? And inside those doors yet more hallways, on and on, ad infinitum.

The fallacy of rites of passage is believing the hallway ever ends. Because the end of one passage is also the beginning of the next. Any certainty footed on reaching the other side of transition will eventually be undermined by the transition following after that. What is life itself but a liminal space between birth and death? Who knows? Maybe death doesn't even have finality? (That's another topic . . . though I've experienced one "sign from beyond" that I have no logical explanation for—Inquire Within.)

As they say, the only constant is change. Each moment is fundamentally transitional: somewhere between day and night, one season to the next, year to year. If no man is an island, than neither is a moment, inextricable from the context of what came before and what will come next. To pin down a man or a moment or an idea to a single point kills the journey we're all on.

DON'T PUT ME IN A BOX

Our culture is not known for its ability to understand nuance, let alone holding conflicting viewpoints in consideration simultaneously. We want certainty. To achieve it, we increasingly slap binary labels on everything from politics (left/right) to class (rich/poor) to personal taste (good/bad). These definitions, meant to help us understand the world, do exactly the opposite. The word 'define' itself comes from the Latin *de fine*, meaning bring to an end—or, to kill. To define something is to kill it.

Society expects that we be one thing. Black or white, gay or straight, man or woman... I ask why it has to be either/or? Why is mixed race identity, bisexual attraction, and transgender existence such a fucking threat? Because people are terrified of liminal space.

I'll put this plainly: definitions serve to kill, but life persists.

LIVING IN THE GRAY

I'm happy to exist in the gray area. I say that now, but the truth is I struggled for a long time to actually do this and mean it. It's comforting to put up those walls, to build yourself a little fortress of impenetrable belief. My therapist put it this way: we're made of water and we're always trying to figure out what glass to pour ourselves into, but sometimes water is meant to spill and flow.

Water doesn't know where it's going. It just goes. We don't know where we're going and we never have, even when we've convinced ourselves otherwise. And that's a good thing. It's the key to living in the present. As the modern proverb goes:

> If you are depressed you are living in the past.
> If you are anxious you are living in the future.
> If you are at peace you are living in the present.

Embracing liminal space is about living in the present. Not here nor there, but *now*. We might call it gray area between black and white, but if you know anything about light, that's where all the color is. Rainbows might seem like a horror flick to some, but not me.

Shine on.

NOTES FROM A CORPORATE SLAVE
A STORY ABOUT SERVICE

Last week I got an email from someone who's been reading my stuff since it was a scattershot blog for the outdoor apparel company I used to own. I knew him as an avid trail runner, a peak bagger, a classic mountain enthusiast. But in this last email he admitted this is only half the picture. "I'm a slave to corporate America," he wrote. "I do it for my wife and kids, and the resentment eats at my soul much worse than the nightly beers eat at my liver and kidneys. But their toll will come..."

His words refused to leave my mind.

On that old blog I used to write stuff like this: We are rebels in a world that wants to cut off our hair and sell us a suit. We turn our back on the idea that $$$ is more than a means to an end. Because we know it's not about the material things we have, but what we do with those things that matters.

Truth was, though, as I wrote these words I also worked in a cubicle compiling title documents for a mortgage company. I rarely discussed this side of my life—why talk about something in which you experience little pride, right?—so when this longtime reader offered such unfettered openness about his predicament, I had to lean into his honesty.

I asked for an interview. And he agreed to go deeper. So sit back . . . as we explore the modern-day fight between freedom and expectation through the eyes of someone who's given 30 years to the corporate world, how we all sometimes wind up inside circumstances we never imagined, and how we might yet escape.

ASCENDING THE LADDER

Tell us what you do . . .

I am a manager of a customer service team for a brokerage firm. The accounts we service may hold all types of securities (mutual funds, bonds, ETFs, stocks, options) and besides handling incoming calls and emails, my team is also tasked with making outbound proactive communications.

How did you get yourself into this position?

I've been working in corporate America for nearly 30 years. As a young newly-wed a year out of college, I just needed to find work. With a BA in English and not being very handy, I wasn't going to be a carpenter or plumber.

It started as a temp job sorting mail. Then I got a full-time offer to join a department that was mostly data entry with some phones. The phones were terrible: long hold times to reach firms you needed information from, incoming calls from irate customers upset about fees or delays. But that job landed me the opportunity for a research position, where I got paid way more to put up with those irate callers, and actually felt some satisfaction in solving their problems.

What promise did you buy into when joining the corporate world?

I bought the classic American Dream. That working diligently effectively translated to upward mobility. At my first company, progress seemed easy: in the course of two years, I nearly doubled my laughable income to something comfortable, and found myself striving for new roles. Generally it took 3-5 months to master each role, then I'd take a new one. It genuinely felt good to provide answers to customers and to help coworkers.

But soon enough I found myself drowning in work delegated to me by my supervisor, maybe a consequence of my persistence. I was newly divorced, so the long hours didn't bother me, the mental exertion becoming a welcome diversion from the emotional turmoil inside. The strain of overwork was drowned in Friday night happy hours that led to even later excursions to clubs. But the bonus paid by the company was more generous than any I'd ever experienced, so I kept going.

Did you ever question the corporate path in the beginning?

During those first years while I rose through the ranks, I had also enrolled in a graduate program in pursuit of the dream of becoming an English professor—but the prospect of driving across town to teach a class at this community college, with no health benefits, and even more schooling (a PhD to obtain) in order to be eligible for a full-time faculty position did not inspire me. I had a more interesting and financially rewarding career at hand.

DISILLUSION SETS IN

How long did the good times last before you realized the corporate gig wasn't what you had imagined?

I've worked for three different Fortune 500 companies without ever leaving my business unit. The first time the company was sold, I found out from a co-worker looking at an online news article. Ten years later it happened again, only this time I was a manager—not that it mattered because still no one told me—and that's when I understood the people working the ranks to make these large corporations flourish are just decimals on a spreadsheet.

You said earlier that resentment eats at your soul. What do you resent, exactly?

I resent the hypocrisy of the ultra-capitalist mission, coupled with the slick, well-applied veneer of humanism. The top executives continue to make more and more money, while the vast majority of employees spend year after year looking at a 2% raise. It's insane to think that the tax liability of some of these executives exceeds the salaries of those whom they employ.

Then something happens in the industry and the layoffs occur. Despite the continual feast and famine cycle of labor, the work still needs to get done, and employees work long days, long weeks, giving up vacation time to make it happen.

Why would I do this? Well, I care about our customers and I take pride in my work. I want to be a person of integrity, someone others can rely upon, and there are all these excellent corporate values to spur me to do my best: BE CLIENT-CENTRIC, OWN IT, COLLABORATE. Yes, I truly believe in all these values but the demands are unsustainable. And the result is that the good people get burnt out over time and leave, making more work for those still around, and the spiral continues.

Why stay corporate then and not find a better-suited path for yourself?

It comes down to comfort, necessity. In my imagination, I always romanticize this idea of living free of material things, able to move on a moment's notice, ever-ready for adventure. But apartments are crowded, noisy places. And there is the dream of home ownership and the promise of the equity you get from it. I bought a townhome and then a house and accumulated stuff. Van life would appeal, but you can't raise kids that way, and it would never appeal to my wife, even if we didn't have kids.

What would it take for you to turn your back on the corporate world now?

I've been trying to figure this out. After my upcoming 30th anniversary of corporate work next year, I don't see any realistic means of leaving this world earlier than 2030, when our youngest son will graduate high school and I'll be 58 years old. For that to happen, either my wife will need to double her income or I'll need to find a second job in the interim (subject to approval by my corporate owner) to provide savings.

I've heard "follow your passion" but my passions are not lucrative. Mountain guides or park rangers don't make enough money to support three kids and a wife who also works part-time to balance family demands with her own career aspirations. And would I enjoy the mountains as much if I were having to cater to clients, make sure they are well-energized and hydrated, properly outfitted, etc.? I've always enjoyed writing, too, but the road to authorship is not a path to readily replace daily wages.

So that leaves other business endeavors, nearly all of which would require new training or education, and starting back from the bottom.

LIVE TO WORK, WORK TO ESCAPE

So, how do you find a sense of escape?

For the past 20 years, my escape has been the mountains. Heck, I even dream about them—I was looking at a map of the San Juans one time and jarringly realized that I was looking for a mountain on the map that wasn't real. In my sleep, I've created a whole mythical sub-range to the east of the Grenadiers sub-range in the real world San Juans. Can you believe that?

What dreams does your corporate gig hold back? What would it take to attain them?

This is an important thing for young adults to think about. What do you want to do? Don't settle down and get a job to save up for those big adventures to do later because you might get to too old to do them.

Life is about choosing your opportunities. Each choice we make acts to open up new opportunities, and simply removes others from the table. Now in my fifth decade, I realize that there are numerous mountaineering experiences I will not have—there is insufficient time and money available due to the choices I've made.

What would you tell someone considering a corporate job now?

I think people need to consider deeply what experiences they want from life, what they want their everyday to be, what they want vacations to be, and milestones, what they want to do by 30, 40, etc. Then, prioritize those things. Figure out what you need to do to attain those visions—because what you have are goals and a goal without a plan is just a dream. Dreams go unrealized unless there is a plan, followed by actions to complete it.

Regularly revisit your dreams and goals, think about your current work, and deliberate on what changes you want to make each year. Don't do it like I did, with regrets and self-loathing and new resolutions each January that go unfulfilled. Just set up a time to check on your plan monthly and make sure you are heading to where you want to be.

WHERE DOES THIS LEAVE US

An old carpenter once told me that construction picks up the people who don't fit in anywhere else. I'll speak for myself, though I imagine it applies to all the carpenters and plumbers I work with, when I say I wouldn't last one day in a cubicle anymore.

Nevertheless, there's a sentiment I sometimes hear on the job, often accompanied by a shrug: *work's work.* When it comes to putting food on the table and paying the bills, sure, work's work. But if it's never more than that, what's the end result?

Does a job like that lead to satisfaction? Or maybe it provides just enough comfort find yourself 30 years down the line, questioning yourself only when it's too late? I don't necessarily have the answers—even if I did they're probably not your answers, anyway.

To paraphrase an idea from the writer Mark Manson on the state of our working lives:

The 20ᵗʰ Century often rewarded emulation over experimentation, with schools, corporations, and institutions favoring conformity over curiosity. Today the tables have turned. Those who challenge assumptions and embrace curiosity are the ones who thrive.

It's never too late to start being curious. Cultivate it. Who knows what might take root.

One final note: almost twenty years ago I quit school to hike the Appalachian trail. A lot of people thought I was crazy—for the record, I went back and graduated—but while I was out there I met an older guy one day who had already set up camp for the night, though it was only lunch time. As I did with most fellow hikers, I asked what had brought him to the trail.

"After forty years of working at the same desk," he said. "I had to do this." Then he searched the sky for a moment before looking me square in my teenaged-eye, adding: "Whatever you do, don't go corporate." With that he retired to his tent, leaving me alone in the middle of the woods, a well-worn footpath before me.

Thanks again to my longtime reader for his openness and honesty.

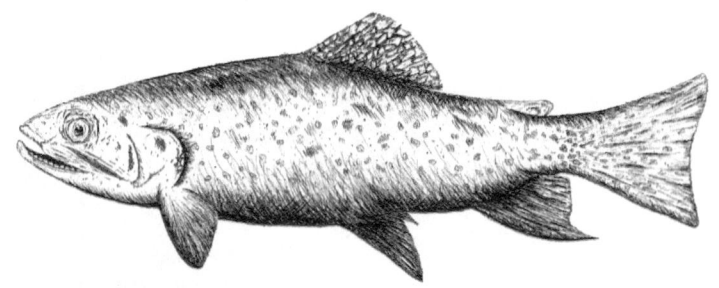

THE FISHERMAN
A SHORT STORY

The fisherman left his phone on the desk and snagged the fly rod from the corner of his cubicle. Standing on the loading dock, he loosened his tie and surveyed the cottonwoods glimmering in the midday sun, casting shadows exactly where he wanted them.

Some days trains idled behind by the building, but today it was quiet. The fisherman climbed the rock bank to the empty tracks and strolled east over the rail ties until he reached the trestle at the creek.

He peeled off the tracks, sliding down the loose gravel, and planted his feet on the sand bar at the water's edge. Resting his rod against a block of concrete, he knelt down and slipped off his loafers, rolling his pants to his knees.

"Yes," the fisherman whispered, closing his eyes as he stepped into the cool water. He unhooked the fly and rolled it into the current, where it dipped and bobbed on the surface into the riffles beneath the shade of the trestle.

After half a minute he pulled the line and recast, threading the fly through the low willows on the far bank. When the fly drifted into an eddy, the brook trout hit.

The fisherman set the hook fast but took his time bringing the fish in, letting it put up an honest fight. Once landed, he admired the sunburst colors in his hand, a red dawn breaking into a night full of stars, a little masterpiece gasping for air.

Sliding the fly from the trout's mouth, he loosened his grip and the fish skittered back to safety. He rinsed his hands, washed the sand from his feet, then slid into his loafers, nodding at the fishing hole before turning toward the tracks.

Back inside the fluorescent office, the fisherman stashed his rod in the corner of his cubicle and checked his phone for what he might have missed.

HOW TO FIX A BROKEN SHOELACE

A STORY ABOUT SELF-RELIANCE

So the other morning I'm pulling on my sneakers, giving the laces a tug, and one of them snaps in two. It's 7am and the frustration piles up.

First, I'm mad at the shoelace for not doing its job. But, alright, things break sometimes, so then I'm mad at myself because I want to throw the damn shoes away, broken laces and all, instead of fixing the problem. Finally, not wanting to own such a ridiculous reaction, I'm mad at our culture for conditioning me to make trash out of perfectly fixable things.

Ah, victimhood. Absolution's finest vintage.

I fish out my old boots from the bin and think back on this pasture gate I once fixed while working as a hand on a cattle ranch in southern Colorado. I had the thing tied up with some baling twine—a temporary fix, no question—when another wrangler came up and said, "when a cowboy fixes things, he fixes them right."

Maybe a little trite, but I never forgot it. So, like an urban cowboy, I went onto Amazon and bought a new pair of laces for my sneakers. And since the color doesn't really match, now the shoes have a little more character than before.

Some might say signs of mending and repair detract from an object, but I think it's proof that a thing has done good work, good enough work that someone has decided it's worth the effort to patch and keep going. We don't need to hide our flaws, do we?

There is a Japanese art form called Kintsugi, or "golden joinery," and in this tradition of fixing broken pottery a craftsman uses a special lacquer mixed with precious metal to celebrate the cracks instead of hiding them. Inseparable from the object, these scars are made beautiful.

Although a patch, golden or otherwise, assumes our ability to fix something in the first place, along with the desire to do so. That's not really what our society is all about anymore. For instance, we now have cars in which you cannot check the oil, even if you wanted to. Self-reliance has been obliterated in the name of reliability. How's that for some capitalistic prophecy?

Yet maybe this has always been the case. Back in 1841, in his essay *Self-Reliance*, Ralph Waldo Emerson said: "The civilized man has built a coach, but has lost the use of his feet."

To think of all we've lost since then.

You could probably make a decent assessment of how lacking in self-reliance we are as individuals by the amount of companies exploiting the deficiency. If you can't cook, DoorDash it; if you can't put an IKEA cabinet together, TaskRabbit shows up—and then maybe you get upset at paying for something you could have done yourself.

Don't get me wrong: it sometimes makes more sense to pay people to do things that you can't or won't do. But I also think it's generally worth knowing *how* to do things, anyway. For the sake of competency, if not quality control.

Except we don't have to know things anymore. Everything we need to know is on the internet. We've outsourced this information and knowledge and experience from our heads to the cloud, and with it our sense of being informed. Call it convenience, call it willful ignorance—tomato tomahto—I include myself in this indictment.

But I think a pushback is coming.

I've been reading about this idea of the New Romanticism. As the writer Ted Gioia explains, the original Romantics in the 1800s were largely pushing away from the mechanization of the Industrial Revolution, the scientific rationalization of nearly everything, for the sake of feeling and emotion, while the New Romantics, right now, are pushing away from the automation of the Technological Revolution, the algorithmic infantilization of our lives, for things more organically conceived and humanly connected.

I say good riddance. Technology will not save us. We can only save ourselves—which means, first, exhibiting a little more self-reliance.

To quote Emerson once more: "For the self-helping man, all doors are flung wide, all tongues greet, all honors crown, all eyes follow with desire. Our love goes out to him and embraces him, because he did not need it."

So much awaits us in that future. But, if nothing else, a self-helping man can at least get himself a new pair of shoelaces.

FIRST YOU ZIG, THEN YOU ZAG

A STORY ABOUT PREDICTABILITY

Even though I'm a writer, I tend to go for music when thinking about creativity. In writing workshops, most people name the best of literati while I'm in the corner dropping obscure references to the Grateful Dead.

This likely has to do with my unrealized desire to be a successful musician. But, also, approaching an idea from a unconventional angle, with a fresh and alternative lens, often reveals things you wouldn't otherwise notice.

So, I do this with writing, but it applies to most of life, as well—by using the widest definition of "creativity." This seems relevant, most of all, when things get stale, a little too predictable, when you need to shake it up and try something different. To offer some musical examples:

After Neil Young recorded his legendary album, *Harvest*, the tastemakers wanted more acoustic songwriting, another 'Heart of Gold.' But Young had other ideas. Instead of recreating the songs that made him world famous, he rejected the pop and later recorded the raw and grungy album, *Tonight's the Night*.

Neil Young has never seemed to care what other people think, and his idiosyncratic styling surely has much to do with his rightful place in music history. But there's another musician who took that penchant for reinvention even further . . . that is, Miles Davis.

Listen to *Kind of Blue* and *Bitches Brew* and try not wonder how the same person made this music. The jazzman famously played with his back to the audience, like some physical manifestation of the music itself—the only other artist I can think of who so radically changed their style time and time again was Picasso—yet, despite the vast differences throughout his career, it always sounded like Miles. One note on his trumpet, especially with that Harmon mute, and you just *know* it's him.

This begs the question: How do you stay authentic through reinvention?

I hate the world authentic. It's been batted around for so long that it's nearly lost all meaning. Nevertheless, here's my definition: Taking a stand while keeping an open mind.

You can't be everything to everyone. Those that try are either lame, phony, or both. That's the whole taking a stand thing. I've always thought that you're doing something right if you rile people up, either for or against you. But that's nothing without an open mind. Those not willing to listen to opposing arguments are ignorant and uninformed. Obviously, that doesn't mean you have to agree; hearing out someone else with a different point of view often serves to strengthen your own convictions. Anyone who is scared to hear something different probably isn't too sure of themselves to begin with.

In other words, authenticity is another way of saying that to figure out who you are you must first cast a wide net, taking in all kinds of experience, blending them together to produce a unique result. A magic potion of sorts—and *we* are the potion.

One more example of musical reinvention:

Bob Dylan—a student of Woody Guthrie, himself a student of countless unknown folk singers he met rambling the country—took this history and formed something entirely his own. He's as authentic as they come. You don't have folkies calling you "Judas!" because you're playing to their wants and desires.

The truth is people know what they know and, generally, just want more of the same. Dylan going electric is the same as Neil Young putting out *Tonight's the Night* and Miles Davis' endless parade of music that redefined jazz. In short, it seems they did it not because they wanted to do it but because they *had* to, understanding that people would catch up sooner or later.

This all makes me think of the line attributed to Henry Ford: If I had asked people what they wanted, they would have said faster horses.

Most people think of horses. Here's to auto-mobiles.

CYCLES
A STORY ABOUT TRENDS

One thing I appreciate about my work as a homebuilder is the tangibility. At the end of the day, I have something which wasn't there in the morning and, if everything goes to plan, will remain for a long time to come. The reality of residential construction, however, is that building a new house often means tearing an old one down, presenting an opportunity to examine other eras of design, memorialized through that same tangibility.

I could talk about the usual suspects: shag carpet, floral wallpaper, popcorn ceilings. Yet, trend du jour aside, I find myself more interested in *why* things come in and out of fashion—why one generation falls in love with something, only for the next to turn their backs on it altogether—and what that might tell us about the things we're building today.

To stick with construction, a friend of mine used to remodel adobe homes in Santa Fe. Picture them: dusty pink exterior, exposed timbers passing through to the inside, lathe-and-plaster walls . . . basic construction. Then comes the invention of drywall, 2x4s shipped from Canada, fiberglass insulation. At first, this is only for rich people, relegating adobe to the "economic" method of building, meaning a lot of those old adobe timbers get covered up. Now, jump to the present and this has entirely reversed. Framed and drywalled homes are cheap. Adobe is expensive (read: back in). And so, in an analog to the suburban practice of pulling carpet from hardwood floors, my friend spent a lot of time ripping drywall from original timber beams.

And this exposes the push-and-pull of which all popular culture is subject: timely vs timeless.

Anything popular must, by definition, be timely. Of the moment, that is, capturing the vibe of the times—TikTok challenges, social outrage, footwear—but time moves fast, evermore so with technology, and if the popularity of these things seems fleeting it's because of the inherent exploitation. When a trend is bandwagoned by every creative on social media, it loses its luster; then it is onto whatever's next, like a cultural hamster wheel taking us nowhere.

But, occasionally, something popular persists long enough to become timeless. As the flow of culture moves onward, it gains meaning, becoming more interesting, especially if it falls in-and-out of favor a couple of times along the way. Timelessness is about respect: respecting a material, a craft, a subject, even an era. It's the simplicity of cooking with quality ingredients and a pinch of salt. It's the minimal finish on a figured piece of walnut. It's the quiet, considered take, not sensationalism.

However, truly great pieces of culture are both timely and timeless. The pursuit of popularity is neither. If a given thing has the goods only, well, time will tell. But as Maya Angelou observed, people may forget what you said or what you did, but they always remember how you made them feel.

That goes for people—but I'd say it goes for trends, too.

ALLEYWAYS, PT. 1
A STORY ABOUT APPEARANCES

My old neighborhood was full of multicolor bungalows. One even had a pair of giant metal bugs mounted on the roof—no H.O.A. in these parts—which meant the streetside views tended to be entertaining, not to mention full of friendly people in their front yards. But whenever I walked the dog I usually chose to veer off the sidewalk altogether, preferring instead to stroll down the alley.

Because, as far as I can tell, the alley is at least twice as interesting as the sidewalk.

You never know what you'll find in the alley. In a small town like mine, it was like a back window into who people really are. Sometimes you'd find a meticulously kept garden, other times a junkyard. Or you'd see those passion projects: people slowly fixing up an old car, maybe assembling a nice backyard collection of kitsch windmills and whirligigs. Whatever the case, those alleys were a treasure trove of raw and unrefined life.

Some say be wary of the alley, that's where you get mugged. But I say be wary of the sidewalk. That's what people want you to see—their best look, their profile picture—a well-curated facade. Curb appeal cannot be trusted.

Alleys have no such agenda. If the sidewalk view is the proverbial smile of a restaurant hostess, the alley is the unglamorous chaos in the back of house. I don't mean that one is more "real" than the other. It's just that of these two sides of the same coin, one is a little more polished.

This reminds me of a course I took in college called the Anthropology of Tourism. The professor talked about the "frontstage" and "backstage" of the places we travel: the former being your resorts, the evening entertainment, the public spaces, the latter being your local haunts, the places tourists don't go.

Sometimes people actively seek out this "authenticity"—the whole tourism vs. traveler thing—and other times you stumble into the backstage without even trying.

This happened to me on a trip to China, after the tour bus stopped at a small-town market beside the Yangtze river. Seeking relief from the fifty other foreigners behind me, I strolled ahead of the pack looking for signs of life that would surely disappear when the mass arrived. Behind a sprawl of exotic vegetables, a flight of stairs went out of sight, and I took them . . . right into the meat market and a hundred pair of eyes staring me down. Butchers held onto their cleavers, stuck in pork bellies as I circled the area, all conversation silent, the locals shooting daggers up until I quietly shuffled back down to the tour group. Uncomfortable would be an understatement.

The backstage is not a welcoming place—not by default, not like the all-inclusive you paid for—but this possibility of discomfort forces us to examine our real and shared humanity and connect beyond some travel-agent experience, beyond some high-gloss rendering of life.

And in the more everyday sense, this is exactly why "connecting" on social media can feel so hollow. Facebook is like the new cul-de-sac, featuring the well-manicured lawns of the digital age. Our personal alleyways are rarely found online because alleyways are where people stash their literal and figurative garbage—not typically something we make an active effort to display.

Our alleys only come to the forefront when we have no other choice, forced by unavoidable circumstance, and when they do, as the saying goes, people come out of the woodwork. All of us have experiences we don't readily share, maybe for fear or guilt or shame, and it's too bad there's a stigma to this. A little more honesty could do humans some good right now. Because we end up caring a whole lot more about each other when we see the alley view alongside that from the sidewalk.

Maybe this is why a place like New York City is so interesting—it has no alleyways. The garbage gets piled on the sidewalk. You can't ignore it. You must see past it, accept it and move on. How else could you have so many people from so many places with so many different histories living side-by-side? To me it's no wonder that NYC is the center of so much cultural conversation. But I'll save that for Alleyways, Pt. 2.

For now, here's to looking beyond the façade.

ALLEYWAYS, PT. 2
A STORY ABOUT NEW YORK CITY

If Alleyways, Pt. 1 was about our personal alleys, then this is what happens when we take those raw parts of our life, normally stashed in the back, and dump them in the front yard. Better out than in, as they say.

A few years ago I was in Manhattan and where better to explore this conversation than a place with no alleyways at all. There's nothing like 75,000 people squeezed into each square mile to amplify human nature— and, specifically, how our physical environment shapes us.

Realists might point out the most visible byproduct of such urban planning: garbage piled on the sidewalk. But I see that as collateral damage to some more fascinating stuff that winds up on the street.

On that trip, after an afternoon meeting spit me out in SoHo, I walked twenty-two blocks back to the hotel, along the way passing: a woman selling vintage paperbacks on a folding table, a heavy metal band thrashing in Alphabet City, chessmen hustling in Union Square, Hare Krishnas chanting with harmonium and bells, and a farmers' market, to name a few encounters. And this says nothing of the one-of-a-kind stores, shops, and restaurants lining every street.

At the outset of the journey, I asked a municipal worker emptying trash bins, "What's a good direction to go?" He said, "Every direction!" Had I taken another path, I have a feeling I'd have written a whole other list just as interesting.

People talk about the *energy* of New York so much so it now seems like a cliché but the place is absolutely electric. I'd say that's directly born from a few million people putting themselves out there, just a sampling of whom I passed on the street, saying to themselves, "Fuck it, let's give it a go."

Because one of the things that often winds up lost in the alley is ambition. Around my small town in Colorado, this could be as mundane as an old Cadillac waiting twenty years for a wrench. Without alleys, though, there is no place to hide yourself or your ideas ... you must act! Forced to expose what otherwise might be stashed in the alley, a quality develops of realness, rawness, truth. In other words, fertile ground for inspiration.

It's no great surprise that so many artists have found their muse in New York: Bob Dylan, Jean-Michel Basquiat, Colson Whitehead, Keith Haring, KRS-One, Patti Smith, Thelonious Monk ... the list goes on and on, forming a cycle of creativity that keeps NYC a cultural bellwether, generation after generation.

But arguably creation, invention, and reinvention have been woven into the fabric of New York City since the beginning. Eager people with novel ideas and unique perspectives have been flowing to and through NYC for centuries.

As a kid, I visited Ellis Island with my family and found my great-grandparents' names in the manifest from the late 1800s. They escaped the pogroms in Russia and found a fresh start stateside, beginning right there in New York harbor.

In this globalized world of today, where we only need wifi to make a video call from another country, it's hard to imagine the kind of cultural distinction coalescing on Ellis Island. A glimpse into this era reveals people emigrating in their finest traditional clothes and it's plain to see they were putting it all out there—and so the tradition continues.

It was the promise of freedom that drew people to New York City a hundred-fifty years ago. The city has never lost that profound sense of possibility. Maybe, behind all the history, it's those missing alleyways which keep it feeling strong. Either way, they certainly put the Statue of Liberty in the right city.

Here's to putting it all out there, alleyways or not.

CHECKMATE IN NEW YORK CITY
A SHORT STORY

Those orange-robed Hare Krishnas are chanting again beneath the Japanese Pagoda tree like the hum in a bad light bulb.

Kaplan barely hears them anymore as he gets to his usual spot in the park, unfolding the legs of his table and plastic chairs. He rolls out his chess board and lines up his chess pieces and scans the people in his corner of Union Square.

Lounging to his right Ellery comes down from the Bronx and slouches in the shade of his yellow and white beach umbrella, drinking a Mexican coke, watching videos on his phone. Doesn't give a shit if he plays, does he? Wasting time, yeh.

And there's Marquez across the path staring down pedestrians under his dew rag and black-on-black Yankees hat. A teenage kid sits down with him and the Dominican pulls his hustling fingers across his thick mustache, moves his pawn, slaps the timer.

Kaplan calls out to a strutting man in a leather jacket. "Play?" The man ignores him and Kaplan flicks his hand. He pulls his bag into his lap and pours vodka and some ginger ale into a paper cup.

Over by the crosswalk Foster is up two pieces on Banks who leans on his hand, tapping his grey goatee. With one eye on the board, Foster hands the second half of his burning cigarette to his old ally Fraelich who sits cross-legged on the ground.

Polished Captain Malley walks through the crowd with a two-cop escort and Kaplan sips his vodka, showing his failing teeth until the shiny cops disappear into the subway.

A casual husband and wife stop walking. The man pulls out one of Kaplan's chairs and sits down. He picks up the queen. This is the queen, you know? What the hell are you doing with the queen? The man turns to his wife, the queen in his hand, who snaps a picture on her phone. The casual man winks at Kaplan before getting up.

A boy sitting on the stone steps across the path gets up and quickly fills the chair. Kaplan tops off his vodka. They go move for move until the boy twists his face. "This makes no sense," Kaplan says. The boy nods and moves his rook. "Just beat me." Checkmate in three and the boy hands over five dollars.

The wind blows his empty paper cup off the folding table and Kaplan flicks his hand, his eyes back on the square.

FIND YOUR

PEOPLE #FYP

ALCOHOL
A STORY ABOUT JUDGEMENT

For the past few months I haven't been drinking very much, more circumstantial than anything, and along the way I've begun noticing an odd thing within myself and in my friends. Seeing that it's now January—Dry January, for some—a few days beyond the overrated reverie of New Year's Eve, it seems like a good time to talk about booze.

I started drinking around freshman year of high school, initially engaging in the classics: skimming shots off random bottles in the liquor cabinet, pilfering an assortment of beers from the fridge, and occasionally pulling "Hey Misters" at the gas station in the next suburb over.

It's safe to say that whatever word best described my relationship to alcohol from the beginning, "healthy" would not be it. Ignoring the abstinence argument foisted upon us by our D.A.R.E. instructor, weekends became debaucherous and sloppy, if not outright dangerous, all in the name of sociability. Because if you weren't drinking, with few exceptions, you weren't cool.

This is the basis upon which my understanding of alcohol was built. And when you're sixteen, or eighteen, or twenty, trying to make friends with people whom mostly grew up understanding alcohol the same way, it's no small wonder why the binge kept going.

I'd like to think that now, in my late thirties, I have the confidence to say no. But then I go to a party and order a tonic with lime in a rock glass just to avoid questions. Some might point out this marks a deep-seated issue . . . yeah, please see the above three paragraphs.

But, like I mentioned, over the past couple of months I haven't been drinking and I've been paying more attention to this idea—not from some conscious effort to understand my history with alcohol, but more a noticing of how I've felt when booze was on the table. Feeling number one: judgement.

Mainly, I judged myself. Case in point: at a work happy hour as everyone sat outside, I went into the bar and ordered an non-alcoholic beer, pouring it into a glass. When, out of friendly curiosity, someone asked what it was, I only said an IPA. Because I thought they cared.

In a separate instance, I brought a few cans of NA beer to dinner at a friend's house. He saw it, nodded, and pulled out a bottle of wine. "Don't judge me," he said. "I want the real stuff tonight." Because he thought I cared.

I've heard it said that drinking is the only drug that makes people think there's something wrong with you if you don't do it. So, the question is if other people don't really care what I'm drinking and I don't care what they're drinking, who exactly is doing the judging?

Drinking has a storied place in our culture. Take Hemingway, for instance, who might be as famous for his drinking as his writing. His stories make you (read: me) want to drink. I had vermouth straight-up for the first time after reading *A Farewell to Arms*. I brought a wine skin into the mountains after finishing *The Sun Also Rises*. So, when I re-routed my road trip honeymoon to visit his grave in Ketchum, Idaho, I figured I'd have a drink there in his honor.

The gravestone itself was covered in bottles—whiskey, wine, beer, vodka— other people toasting the man. But I didn't end up having that drink. Instead I stood there for ten minutes and left. In retrospect, the place perfectly captures our collective ambivalence about alcohol, because sitting there amongst the bottles of booze was a coin, and when I knelt down for a closer look, I saw it was a token from Alcoholics Anonymous—24 hours sober.

Next to a figure like Hemingway, a celebrated drunk, perhaps the nagging feeling of judgement which accompanies drinking is deflected. I certainly didn't feel guilty about forgoing a toast. Yet even the founding fathers of this country wrestled with the internal conflict brought on by alcohol. Benjamin Franklin once wrote: "Wine is proof that God loves us, and loves to see us to be happy." While elsewhere, in his autobiography, he aspired to be *temperate in his pleasures,* writing: "Eat not to dullness; drink not to elevation."

In other words, to use the cliché, everything in moderation. And what is moderation if not simply having alternatives? I've certainly had role models in my life who abstained from alcohol. My grandmother, for one, was always the life of the party and I saw her drink exactly one sip of champagne; likewise, my grandfather always quit after a single glass of Merlot. But those wholesome examples were often obscured by the persuasive sound of peer-pressure chanting, "Drink this beer dude!"

However, the malted tide seems to be ebbing. There are dedicated non-alcoholic bars out there, dozens of companies making non-alcoholic beer. Sobriety is, dare I say, kind of trendy.

One of my best friends has been sober for nine years, providing a lot of time to think on these things, and I was talking to him about all of this the other day. At one point he asked: how often do people who don't actually want to drink go out and do it anyway? *A lot* is the answer.

Returning once more to judgement. Why do we drink, or even pretend to drink, when we'd rather not? Personally, I think it's my twenty-year-old self in there still convinced that if you're not drinking, you're not cool. But you know what I have to say to him now . . . fuck off kid.

The past doesn't quiet so easily, after all. Especially if you don't have something better to run toward. Ironically, it's a childhood vice that offers me at least some kind of answer.

Recently, a few of my friends came down from a day of rock climbing, debating where to grab some beers, the normal post-climb play, but then one of them suggested ice cream. Turns out none of them actually wanted to drink anyway. So instead of going to the bar, they went to the ice cream shop.

Maybe in the end the key to quieting our twenty-year-old self is by hanging out with our eight-year-old self instead. Either way, here's to some judgement-free beers—and ice cream socials.

LOSING THE CHILI COOKOFF
A STORY ABOUT FIRST IMPRESSIONS

I consider myself a decent cook. While I have no fancy tricks, can't make sauces or bake, I regularly turn out good meals that don't necessarily come out of a box or the freezer (no offense, my frozen fish stick dinners, I will always love you). So when it came to the chili cookoff last month, I thought I stood a decent chance of doing well. When they tallied the votes, however, I was shocked to place . . . dead last.

Tenth of ten, bottom of the barrel, the worst. I sulked in my chair while the judging concluded, staring down the little paper cups with those other, superior chilis spread before me. And I asked myself, where did it all go wrong?

Forgoing the nuances of competitive chili cooking technique, of which I'm clearly no authority, I think the answer is simple: context, or how the situation we're in at any given moment shapes our initial perception of everything. In other words, this is about first impressions.

We're social animals, after all, and making snap judgements is our ancestral survival instincts kicking in—which holds true whether you're deciding if an unknown person is friend or foe, or in matters of literal taste. If something tastes bitter, maybe it's poisonous. Does a thing smell of rot? Well, then, it might make you sick.

I'm not implying that my last-place chili was bitter and/or rotten. But let's explore what people *do* like, as a matter of taste, when something hits our tongue. And we might as well use one of the most famous taste tests of modern times: The Pepsi Challenge.

This was Pepsi's major offensive against Coke in the Cola Wars of the 80's and 90's. In a blind taste test, participants would try a sip of each brand. More often than not, Pepsi won. This was great for marketing, obviously, even if the results were unceremoniously skewed by our natural bias for sugar. Because the "sweet tooth," as it were, derives from our evolution as hunter-gatherers, when high-energy foods like honey were major sources of nourishment. So you can blame that unshakeable love of ice cream on instinct.

A sip test like the Pepsi Challenge, as writer Malcom Gladwell points out in his book *Blink*, tilts the scale toward the sweeter soda—even when a person would prefer the less sweet soda if drinking the entire can.

My conclusion: first impressions lie.

Other studies have shown it takes only one-tenth of a second for someone to form their first impression of another person. This isn't simply superficial. Traits like trustworthiness, competence, likeability, aggressiveness, attractiveness are all decided in that time—a lot to consider within a few milliseconds.

I wonder how often our first impressions lead us astray from people, places, and things we might actually connect with. For instance, I am generally quiet when I meet new people; I like to take in the situation, observe rather than assert myself. Sometimes people think I'm an asshole because of it. Now, I don't think I'm an asshole (I also don't think I'm a bad cook, so who knows), yet it might have cost me a few potential friendships over the years.

The epitome of this half-baked judgement lands in the digital realm: scrolling. Whether it's swiping left or ripping through Instagram Reels, how much gets overlooked simply because it didn't catch our attention in the moment?

Sometimes you need to hear and read and see things two, or three, or six times before you *get* it. And when this happens, you're so often hit in a more profound and lasting way than the quick dopamine rush provided by a positive first impression.

Books are like this. Sometimes they start slow, until they catch and you literally can't put the thing down. We'd miss that if, after a couple of pages, we stopped reading. I heard a rule once about how to give books a proper chance: commit to reading the first hundred pages, minus your age. I like this; also, I think the idea applies far beyond books.

When you're young, you have more time to see if your first impressions are right or not. And it's worth exploring these perceptions, when you have the time, so that when you're old you don't have to waste it on things you surely don't like. My grandmother wasted no time at all on things she didn't care for, seemingly able to cut through those first impressions to what lay beneath; and she suffered no fools because of it.

If you're stuck on surface-level perspective, your reality might be equally shallow. So go beyond—drink the whole can. However, since first impressions will always be there, I have one applicable note on making chili: don't be too spicy.

This probably goes for people, too.

DRESS CODE VIOLATION

A STORY ABOUT COSTUMES

I am currently in the middle of a road-trip through New England: ten days of camping along the Maine coast, bookended by formal weddings in Newport, Rhode Island and Cape Cod. Which means one side of the suitcase contains my tux and suits and the related accoutrements of such occasions; while on the other side, it's bandanas and flannels and all the gear necessary to mess around in the woods for a stretch. If the TSA had searched my bag, they likely would have been left wondering—and, frankly, that's the way I like it.

For better or worse, the things we wear tell people who we are. Look no further than a doctor guesting on some daytime television talk show. There is no other reasonable explanation for them wearing scrubs on set, as they certainly didn't just walk out of the operating room, except that a doctor in a suit-and-tie doesn't look the part enough. So a producer says wear scrubs and everyone instantly gets it: this is a medical expert. Strip everyone naked and people cannot tell you so much about themselves.

In a way, clothes are like costumes. After all, we feel differently when we have on different outfits. Work clothes, leisure clothes, formal wear reflect the various sides of ourselves and, consciously or not, we're always putting them on display. And isn't our notion of a "costume" simply an outfit taken to the point of caricature? Dial it back and you might just call it part of your wardrobe.

Maybe this is why Halloween has always been my favorite holiday. People—myself included—often bring out sides of themselves they otherwise don't or won't. Put the mask on to take the mask off, you know, as the chance to be somebody else is the perfect opportunity to be your real self. (Considering I've been a cowboy the last ten years running, you think I'd take the hint at what I should be doing with my life.) But this isn't about one night in October. It's an everyday idea. This is about using clothes to bring out parts of yourself which you like.

I am no fashionista, but I once owned an apparel company—hats and tee shirts, mostly, for people who climb and ski—and when you spend all day thinking about selling clothes, inevitably you come up with some justification for showing up. This copy (lifted from the now defunct website) sounded like:

> "Sometimes at the old office, I'd put on a shirt worn around the campfire beneath my button-down. It made me think of being out there. Because I've always thought clothes can connect you to those different parts of life. Like that hat you wear on every climb, the tank you always do yoga in, and the sweater you put on at every campfire. They take on this meaning that's deeper than a piece of apparel."

I don't sell clothes anymore but I still buy that. I'm sure we all have at least one item in the closet that means more because of the accumulated experiences we've had while wearing it. Even hanging in there quietly, no longer in use, it's a personal artifact with more visceral potential than a photo on the wall will ever bring. To me, that's a case for squirreling away a few choice items to dig up in old age, for when you need a reminder of the real living you've done. As Bill Perkins explains in his book *Die With Zero*, we retire not only on money, but on experiences and memories, too.

So, forget fast fashion and hang onto your clothes long enough to thread some stories through them. I am pretty sure that after a week of being sandwiched amongst campfire-laden sweaters and flannels, my tuxedo will have gained some extra flavor. And you can bet I'll be thinking about it next time I get gussied up for another black tie affair.

THE INFLUENCER'S UNENVIABLE LIFE
A STORY ABOUT FINDING YOUR PEOPLE

A friend of mine recently got close with a well-known influencer—a person with all the markers of success: hundreds of thousands of followers, high six-figure income, complete digital nomad—but as soon as the accolades wore off, it became clear I wouldn't want his life at all.

The guy travels the world, reads his poetry for live audiences. On the surface it looks great. He consults with paying clients and has "friends" everywhere he goes, which I put in quotes because the truth is he spends a lot of his time alone. And, in a word, seemed to be incredibly lonely.

Those clients, they're all virtual—funneled in from Instagram—and as many of us know by now, there's that moment when you get off a video call, especially after a lively discussion and it's suddenly so quiet. In that harsh juxtaposition, you can't deny that those people on the other side weren't actually there with you at all.

I won't harp on this guy because he obviously cannot defend himself, but I *will* argue against his main premise that the path to freedom, financial or otherwise, is found through social media. Don't get me wrong: I understand the need for branding and business development. What I take issue with is the incessant corruption of your art, your personality, of your life itself for the sake of *content*.

In this mindset, the façade you end up creating is thin and weak. Before long, it's hard to even make sense of your original premise. Just as the cobbler's kids have no shoes, the wellness influencer so often seems to be lacking in the very wellness they promote.

That used to be called selling out. Though as avenues to find job security in every field dry up, selling out almost seems necessary—so it's hard to take issue with the idea wholesale—the important difference is that selling out doesn't mean you need to sell yourself out, too. So let's make a distinction and rally around those fighting with integrity, staying true to themselves, and instead call out those influencers who corrupt themselves daily for the feed.

Because if everything in life is done to support content creation, then what's the point? Where's the actual living? Many reports from influencers, TikTokers and YouTubers, say the gig has almost ruined their lives, riddling them with anxiety, yet they cannot stop because the algorithm requires such complete allegiance that to turn away in any meaningful capacity would mean digital punishment.

As they say, though, misery loves company. So is it any wonder that most of these influencers and the companies that pedal their schtick are out there trying to convince us that we really, truly, dearly need to be on the socials for our own sake?

I had a revelation the other day: I don't want be on social media because I don't need social media. After months, maybe even years of not feeling that it's serving me, the clarity was shocking. And I'm not the only one. I've been having more and more conversations with people about abandoning social media altogether.

It's all rather unfortunate, too, because I recall a time when getting on Facebook meant connecting with actual friends, people you knew in real life, when the platform itself merely extended the relationships you already had. This functionality is still buried in there somewhere, which I glimpsed fleetingly after I wrote about getting divorced—it led to great exchanges with some old friends—but the friendships that once persisted online have increasingly been replaced by influencers and their followers.

The reality of our modern online relationships is that they are incredibly weak. Think about it this way: if the power goes out, will the relationship still be there? If the answer is *no*, then maybe it's not worth as much as you think. Perhaps this is why modern friendship can feel so lonely.

Much of it feels like a performance. The heart is the perfect symbol for our online affection because it's our hearts that are affected when we give and receive likes. Consider the inane things we do to stay relevant: join ridiculous challenges, corrupt ourselves for content, pretend we're fighting for something, for a cause, by making an Instagram post "in solidarity" when it doesn't actually move the needle except for in our own minds. We've all been infected with the idea that the online world can supplant the real thing.

A digital community—while a community it may be—doesn't hold a candle to the connections we make in person. I'm not some luddite saying we shouldn't be online, but that this space should be transitory, used as needed, an avenue to initiate connections in order to foster them elsewhere, in person.

I'm grateful for my actual friends, the people I have chosen and who have chosen me, and I don't mind cutting off the "friends" online.

It's funny to me that one way to find the happiness, the groundedness, that settled and satisfied and fulfilled life which influencers love selling is by getting rid of these people altogether. I don't live my life for the *content*, but to be content. I'm not trying to surround myself with people who make me feel inadequate—and influencers, by and large, profit off doing just that.

Perhaps this whole rant is ironic coming from someone trying to make a living writing, much of it online. But I like to think if you've read this far, you get it. You share this sensibility of what's important. And you know that finding the good stuff in life is not always where people say it is. Some of it is online—alright—but for the most part, it's not.

To wrap this up, it was my birthday the other week. All I know is that I'd take a handful of friends who call and text over a hundred that tap out *HBD!* on my Facebook wall. And that will never change.

So here's to high fives and handshakes, hugs and kisses, and all the things you will never be able to do through a screen.

STAYING ANALOG IN THE DIGITAL AGE

A STORY ABOUT TANGIBILITY

This starts with the terrible noise of an alarm clock—and by that I mean my phone—jolting me awake each morning, into consciousness and an already-endless stream of notifications. And like that, I'm in it . . . the digital shitstorm that is modern life.

Eventually, however, having suffered this enough, I purchase a clock, an actual clock, an analog clock with nice music instead of that rasping alarm. Not to be hyperbolic or anything, but it honestly changed my life.

Turns out the artist who designed the clock, Jamie Kripke, lives in my town and invited me to his studio where he explained the whole reason he made the thing was to get away from this exact kind of digital intrusion. And as we sat around talking, it almost felt, dare I say, subversive.

It might seem absurd to call a clock subversive, but when opting out of the internet is considered counterculture, having a clock that is simply a clock goes against the current of society. Perhaps this is a case for simplification, a stand against multitasking. Even if a device *can* do multiple things well, maybe it's still preferable to have a device that does only one thing. Why?

I'll answer with a story.

When I got divorced, the first thing I took were my vinyl records. One night my brother called and asked about my plans that evening. "Listening to a record," I said. "That's it?" he asked. "That's it," I said.

Call me old fashioned but that constituted a solid evening. With no notifications pulling me elsewhere, I could just be *there*. The turntable spinning like a dharma wheel, right into the now. This is the beauty of disconnecting.

Physical media keeps the door closed to outside intrusions, which in a way means going off the grid, although that makes me think about disappearing into some cabin in the woods and this is something more universal. Because sometimes disconnecting happens right in the living room: the phone somewhere else on silent, a record playing, good food cooking in the cast iron pan. You're there.

The author and poet Gertrude Stein once wrote about her hometown: "There is no there there." Meaning her childhood memories still existed in her mind, yet the place that produced them had long since disappeared. The opposite of this is true, as well, and perhaps even more relevant, as we often long for something that never existed in the first place. We feel the *there* of a memory as if it had been real, but in fact it's merely a figment of our imagination—fantasies created from snips and snaps of vicariously lived experiences, compounded evermore by our digital lives, courtesy of shared photos and videos and texts and DMs. This is the false promise of a digital utopia.

Because the only real *there* is here . . . *here*. For the digital world, by definition, is always elsewhere. Watching someone absentmindedly walking down the street while staring at their phone, you know this. You know it, too, because the instant your own screen goes dark, it's like you've been transported back to the present from another dimension. And what happened to that last hour?

This is part of why I like building houses for a living. One of my favorite things is rolling up to the jobsite and hearing the stonemasons tinking away with their chisels. It's a sound humans have been making for thousands of years. I feel quite confident saying the digital realm and AI will never touch that occupation.

And I think this sense of return to earlier times is widely felt. Consider the rise of #cottagecore: baking bread, crafting, homesteading, the fame of Ballerina Farm. It speaks to something we all crave in this modern world . . . tangibility.

Allow me to return again to records. I once found a trunk of old 78 rpm records in my grandfather's basement, a time capsule that even included recordings of him and his brothers and sisters from the 1950s. Do you think a Spotify playlist will last that long?

In this digital world, where everything gets buried in the 1s and 0s after existing for ten minutes, staying analog means taking up a different kind of space—a space that leaves us vulnerable to the kind of imperfection that fundamentally makes us human.

For all the potential of digital connection, it still feels cheap compared to the real, sometimes awkward, in-person interactions. The emotions produced in these tangible spaces linger long after the moment leaves. Can we really say the same about those connections mediated through a screen?

This reminds me of those old Bob Dylan albums, laid down live in the studio and hardly touched up post production. They're imperfect in so many ways, and that's exactly why they're perfect. When you listen to them—really listen to them—you hear all that humanity.

Which brings me back to records for the final time. Jamie Kripke, the clock-designing artist, also hosts "listening parties" where he spins vinyl and everyone simply listens, no conversations, no distractions. It's an exercise in being there and nowhere else.

"That's it?" you might ask. "Yeah, that's it," I say.

I attended one last month. The first thing everyone did upon arrival was put their phones into a wicker basket. The music was great, but that might have been my favorite moment of the night.

Here's to keeping it analog.

OWL FEATHERS
A SHORT STORY

Two owls lived in the rafters of Jim Casey's barn. The barn sat beside two-hundred acres of grama grass prairie, wild, and kept that way by five generations of the oil man's family. Hunting grounds, as they were, for spring turkey and autumn grouse, which kept his dinner table full year-round, and for the owls, a land ripe with field mice awaiting the picking.

Jim Casey knew the owls hunted the prairie because of the piles of small bones littering the dusty floor of his barn. He liked that his land supported them. Before climbing into his truck each morning, he peered into the rafters through the dawn twilight to see them home from another night's hunt.

A feather lay on the dash of the oil man's truck, one that he had collected from amongst the bones on the dusty floor of his barn, and he often pulled his callused fingers down the plumage, watching it fold down and spring open the same way the land did with the seasons.

By then, April had tempered the bitter chill in the air, readying the foothills for long summer days—yet, by all accounts, Jim Casey's mind remained stuck in the hoarfrost of deep winter.

Extraction figures from his competitors drilling in the Bakken forced his company to scrape together barrels just to keep up, and barely at that. He needed more wells. He needed more deals. Without some kind of break, his boys would soon be headed for the unemployment line.

Sometimes Jim Casey looked to the owls in his rafters for solace. Theirs was a simple life, he reckoned. Their instincts hadn't been saddled by responsibility and dulled by convenience, like most men he knew.

But a man needs more than instinct to make it in this world, and when Jim Casey's instincts didn't prove enough he at least had the stubborn try to survive the rest. The hard skin on his hands hadn't gotten that way for nothing.

Having fought through oil gluts, drilling bans, and leaks at old wells, he needed only the courage to do something he knew to be profane. Staring out his kitchen window with a strong and early cup of coffee, Jim Casey made the call: he would drill his two-hundred acre hunting grounds.

The process kicked off like a rifle. His surveyors drove their stakes into his soil. His excavators pulled their gravel road across his prairie. His drill rig bored deep into the earth and his boys got the oil flowing. And soon, Jim Casey found the numbers in his ledger book rising.

At dawn, he peered into the rafters of his barn and found the two owls missing. He chewed on his tongue and stared at their vacant perch. Jim Casey turned his back. Didn't have much of a choice, he reckoned.

When the oil man got into his truck, he pulled his callused fingers down the feather on his dash. His hard skin hadn't gotten that way for nothing.

HOW TO GET
USED, PROPERLY
A STORY ABOUT BOUNDARIES

Kurt Vonnegut once wrote: "The worst thing that could possibly happen to anybody would be to not be used for anything by anybody." In other words . . . being useless.

Although, the alternative to this, getting used in the worst sense, isn't much better. Thankfully there's a lot of room on the spectrum between full-on people pleaser and total deadbeat. It seems the trick is finding that sweet spot in the middle, which leaves us with the question—how to get used, properly?

Do you remember that show *Locked Up Abroad*, where people got caught smuggling drugs across international borders, winding up in hellish prisons far from home? Wild stories. And useful here in addressing the first part of the equation of how to get used: who and what are we serving?

Accepting the role of drug mule is clearly a poor usage of your personal service. The justification almost always came down to money, and money is often reason enough to get used—it certainly pushes plenty of people off to their miserable jobs every morning—but along with money hopefully you're also serving something greater. For instance, God.

I mainly bring God into this conversation because it epitomizes justification for all kinds of behavior. The benevolence of your Mother Teresas, the viciousness of your Crusades. Justification is the most powerful force out there. You don't have to believe in God to understand this. The least we can do is be honest about the *why* behind our actions, and who stands to benefit.

Because, regardless of the final recipient, we as individuals feel the joys and the pains of our choices first and foremost. Hopefully these decisions aren't derived from coercion alone, resulting in some personal fulfillment and sense of purpose, as well. After all, having agency in our personal affairs is the key to getting used properly.

As proof, I'll offer two words: yes / no.

There's a lot of talk these days about the power of saying yes—hell, I've written about it myself—but if *yes* enjoys current status as an unstoppable force, then *no* is the immovable object which ultimately keeps us grounded. So be careful with your *yesses* and *nos*.

If you don't balance your *yesses* with healthy boundaries, you'll definitely get used. But if you're consistently saying *no*, then you're relegating yourself to the sidelines of life, slowly becoming useless. The magic happens when a *no* blocks out the unwanted asks upon your time, holding space for your *yes* to shine.

We get used to the extent we're willing to let ourselves get used. Own this truth.

I think about it like this: saying *yes* to anything means saying *no* to something else, something we might actually prefer. When I'm scrolling through a bunch of entertaining bullshit on my phone, I'm not reading or writing or looking at the trees or spending time with people I care about. The choice isn't always easy, but it's still a choice. And when I feel guilty in my choosing, I know I've made the wrong one.

It's worth repeating: we get used to the extent we're willing to let ourselves get used. But in the end, if you've got your reasons behind you, your *yesses* and *nos* in order, then fuck it, get used and enjoy it.

DOOMSDAY PREPPER CONVENTION: A FIELD REPORT

A STORY ABOUT COMMUNITY

A sign cropped up alongside the road: *Prepper Convention*. Doomsday preppers, that is, as in people preparing for the apocalyptic collapse of society and how one might survive it.

I had to go.

The county fairgrounds often host eclectic gatherings where enthusiasts of dairy goats, quilts, guns, show horses, and antiques find their people—as do those at the regular Saturday farmers' market—so these survival isolationists queuing up next to the livestock corrals wasn't entirely unusual.

To set the scene inside the exhibit hall, I'll catalogue a few of the vendors:

1. Bunker design plans
2. Off-the-grid solar setups
3. Non-perishable food supplies
4. WWII paraphernalia
5. Hand-sewn EMF radiation blocking hats
6. Beef jerky / hot sauce

7. A long table of weaponry, starting with knives and transitioning upward to machetes, swords, battle axes, medieval maces, morning stars and flails

Clearly, multiple cultural circles meet in this Venn diagram. In their basic practicality, a lot of it makes sense; taken to the extreme (the default context within the convention) . . . well, diminishing returns.

The prime survival mechanism which has gotten humans so far in this world is that we strive to understand the unknown, an innate desire unlike that of any other creature, and why we have myths, legends, religion, science, conspiracies. These things help us make sense in a nonsensical world and, historically, these shared stories have brought us together. At the prepper convention, however, you see just the opposite.

One of my best friends says there are two kinds of people in this world: those that think *me*, and those that think *we*. Anthropologists describe modern societies on a spectrum between "individualist" and "collectivist"—essentially, *me* vs. *we*. America falls on the individualist end, to the extreme. After all, we love the self-made man, the hardworking individual who goes it on his own and finds success. So is it any wonder that when we consider the end of society, the vision drawing crowds is that of survival in isolation?

As David Petersen writes in his book *Heartsblood*: "Cities create crowding, crowding promotes estrangement, strangers spread fear, fear breeds contempt." It's the contempt in our modern world which bothers me. And I left the prepper convention bothered that so many people, in a doomsday scenario, are dead set on isolating themselves as far from everyone else as possible. Because to spend a lot of time preparing for societal collapse is a bit of a self-fulfilling prophecy, and when you see everything through the lens of a doomsday scenario, life can look a little grim.

Then again, maybe all the non-perishable survival fare had me hungry.

It was Saturday and as I walked out of the exhibit hall tents from the farmers' market spread across the parking lot. Staring at the fresh vegetables it hit me that, should the apocalypse come, I could either hide away in some bunker living off four-hundred cans of corned beef hash. Or I can find some good people, build a community, grow some food, and survive like us humans have forever.

Make the choice: *me* vs. *we*

POLITICAL YAKAMOOCHI*

A STORY ABOUT PARTY AFFILIATION

Here's a true story about some people who divided themselves and ruined everything good they ever had. Am I referring to our modern state of affairs? No, I'm talking about Easter Island: the remote Polynesian outpost with those famous stone heads called the Moai.

Archaeologists generally agree the story goes like this: a seafaring people arrive on a lushly forested island and start carving Moai to honor their ancestors. As the population grows the trees dwindle and with less natural resources tribal warfare ensues. Each clan carves more Moai, vying for the favor of their ancestors. The continued infighting leaves the island indefensible against an outside attack and sure enough European explorers eventually show up on the island's shores. After that, complete collapse.

The Moai still stand today, a big tourist attraction—monuments to the tribalism that destroyed the island (though that's probably not on the brochure).

This all happened on the most remote inhabited island on the planet. But you know who understood these perils just as well? George Washington. Seventy-four years after Europeans arrived on Easter Island and five-thousand miles away, Washington delivered his farewell address, having voluntarily given up the presidency after only two terms. In it, he said:

> "Let me now warn you in the most solemn manner against the baneful effects of the spirit of party . . . it agitates the community with ill-founded jealousies and false alarms, kindles the animosity of one part against another, foments occasionally riot and insurrection. It opens the door to foreign influence and corruption, which finds a facilitated access to the government itself through the channels of party passions."

Some triggering words in there. You feel those party passions?

Now—I'd like to pause here—to point out that Washington wrote this in 1796, long before our modern political parties were a glimmer in some hungry politician's eye. Washington's whole speech is worth reading (if you don't mind some dense language), but it seems to me the main moral of the story is that whatever side you're on we must be increasingly wary of that *spirit of party*.

As the ancient Easter Islanders might tell you, devotion to tribalism is a one-way ticket to societal destruction. Their Moai stand in commemoration of that truth. But we're building statues these days, too.

Rather than stone, though, our monuments are made of flesh. As the islanders imbued their statues with honorific magic, so do we deify our politicians—talisman shaped not by hammer and chisel but by the desire to see our most fervently held beliefs come to life.

Except that, for the most part, I don't think that is actually true. Most people don't worship politicians. And yet, based on the news coverage from nearly every angle, mainstream or otherwise, you would be hard-pressed to believe that's not the case.

However, like the Moai, politicians are merely vessels for the power that *we the people* give them.

In other words, it's hard to blame the politicians in a representative democracy for doing their job—representing us. These figureheads are merely condensed and compacted versions of ourselves, contradictory, confused, and fickle as any individual, multiplied by a few million voting constituents. You cannot blame the Moai for people carving them into being and you can't blame the politicians for how we've crafted them, either. *Of the people* isn't some bullshit phrase.

But if you take away the politicians, then what is left but us, our party passions burning, clan against clan in a zero-sum game? As George Washington said, this is a dangerous road we travel.

So what can we do about it?

What we do as individuals drives what we do as a people. If we want a civil society, then that will take civility on a personal level. I've written before that I work with a large cross-section of society which means, among other things, interacting with a wide-ranging set of political viewpoints. On the job, we are there for the common goal of building a fine house—and that allows us to see beyond our differences for the sake of the greater good.

Whether it's building a house or building a country, it's the *we* versus *me* attitude that matters. Not to say we ought to agree on what the end vision looks like, but a well-meaning discussion footed in curiosity not animosity will get us a whole lot closer to building the kind of homeland we all want.

By the way, you know what happens to tradesmen who decide they want to be assholes on my jobsite? They get fired. And I'm convinced that most people on the internet should be fired for being assholes in this national conversation. Maybe then politicians wouldn't be such assholes, either.

But again, this starts with us as individuals. So my unsolicited advice: get off the fucking phone and the internet and talk to someone in real life who might think differently than you. Find something in common—it's there!—and if you feel yourself thinking this is a lost cause, remember the Moai.

We're either going to build a real community here or keep building statues. And by now we know damn well where the latter leads.

*Learned this phrase from the conductor of a miniature children's train in Naples, Florida.

AMERICA GETS BATTERED . . . AND DEEP FRIED

A STORY ABOUT SOLIDARITY

I expected carnies. This is my idea of the county fair—carnival showmen, slightly punkish, Barnum and Bailey's with a touch of *Ripley's Believe It or Not!*—and we saw a six-foot, bean pole of a man blowing up balloons for the dart throw, a bucktoothed bald man shagging ping-pong balls for the win-a-goldfish game, and some incredible handlebar mustaches. Yet, oddly enough, the ride jockeys operating the Ferris wheel and Tilt-a-Whirl were clean-cut Mexicans in company polo shirts . . . corporate carnies, who would have thought?

Thankfully, the crowds more than made up for any deficit in interesting people. Young and old, urban and rural, white, black, brown, carnies, cowboys, hippies: a real cultural convention, a true taste of America.

Of course, the carnival is only one part of the county fair. Beside the funnel cakes and turkey legs stood an exhibit hall and livestock pens full of prize-winning chickens, rabbits, goats and pigs, and a handful of beaming kids from the 4-H club who raised them. While on the other end of the fairgrounds, for proper juxtaposition, roared the demolition derby.

Demolition derby . . . possibly the most American thing. Imagine its conception! "Hey, buddy, let's smash these old cars together until the last one's standing. Yeeewwww!!!" The derby kicked off with a sequined cowgirl slamming a sledge hammer onto a contestant's hood before a team of Mad Max vehicles charged into one another, fire, smoke, and engine fluid leaking across the dirt arena. Pure entertainment. You could draw a throughline straight from the gladiators in the Roman Coliseum to this spectacle, the type of thing that has gotten people excited for millennia.

A juxtaposition, indeed. Because for all the over-produced, buffed-and-polished entertainment served up these days, the county fair still hangs onto a certain downhome charm: this DIY attitude, quintessentially American, which has kept it an annual staple in towns throughout the country for over a century. It's a *feeling* more than anything. The derby, the livestock show, and every carnival game has it, this allure of the chance for recognition, unconventional as it may be, and I must ask: is that so different from the American dream?

"You'd be the youngest in history," the carnie told my eight-year-old son who insisted on trying the milk bottle toss. Of course, he lost his $10 in thirty-seconds. Sullen, he seemed to understand as I explained the grift—that they make it look easy, though it's nearly impossible—so when we reached the basketball toss at the next booth, he begged me to try that one, too.

You could tell which stuffed animal prizes had been hanging around longest from the dust coating their fur, and the carnies had a habit of slapping them clean on a knee before rewarding the lucky winners, which had people lining up to try their hand. Appropriately enough, the grandest prize of all was a giant stuffed corndog—though it would have taken a Powerball-worthy string of luck to take that home.

As the night settled in and the lot dust caught the rainbow lights of the rides spinning overhead, I watched all of these different people enjoying the midsummer evening and couldn't help thinking how wholesome it felt. Such a contrast to the big circus peddled to us these days, on the news and damn near everywhere else.

Too much. It's all a bit too much. Ah, but maybe the county fair provides a chance for relief from such woes.

There's an upstart print newspaper, conceived during the isolation of the pandemic, called County Highway. I say it features the most interesting American writing happening today. As they explain, the county is "a chunk of earth big enough to allow for a variety of human types, but small enough to get to know a decent number of your neighbors, where they come from, what they're proud of, what they fear, what they smoke, what they drink, and what they love. Counties are the right-sized places for telling stories."

Based on what I saw walking around the county fair, that feels right.

Here's a hot take: I don't think we're supposed to be so connected. Endless notifications, barrages of emails and texts, every product new and used at our fingertips, even the self-evident convenience of FaceTiming halfway around the world—these things, situated within the context of globalization, have been sold to us as some kind of utopia, but what if they are actually making everything worse?

Instead of thinking bigger, perhaps we need to think smaller. Maybe that looks like people focusing on what's in front of them—not on a screen— communities becoming more self-sufficient, relying more on local goods and services, local agriculture, supporting small business. If not entirely sustainable, it seems like a good start.

For one example: the last few years I've bought into a farm share and, for the length of the growing season, pick up a weekly box of vegetables from this young farming couple a few miles from my house. Who knows if that makes a tangible difference in the world, but there's something special about knowing the people who grow your food.

So, perhaps the future looks much like the past: reveling in simple pleasures. Maybe as a culture we're approaching that simplicity on the other side of complexity. I'll only say that when I see a few thousand people of all different stripes enjoying a summer night at the county fair, well, I can't help thinking we might be doing alright.

WON'T YOU HAVE
A CIGARETTE?

A SHORT STORY

The text said: *BRING DINNER HOME. YOUR FATHER'S HERE.*

Every few months it happened like this. Luanne's old man pulled his long-haul rig through Chattanooga to bother her and her mom like they were a regular family. The last time he'd sat himself right back at the head of the table, starting in with his questions before dinner was even served.

"You got a job?" he asked Luanne.

"Yes."

"You got a boyfriend?"

"What do you care?"

"Because I'm asking."

She twisted her shirt tail beneath the table. "No, I don't have a boyfriend."

"Hmm." He sipped at his beer. "You some kind of queer?"

Didn't take long for Luanne to remember why she hated him. She always dug back. "How's living in your truck, dad?"

It had only been half an hour since her shift began, but Luanne took a cigarette break anyway. Walking onto the loading docks, she pulled a Red from a crumpled soft pack and read her mother's text again.

"Got another?" the tramp asked.

Luanne jumped at his voice, played it off with a small laugh. These freight train riders had come around before. Her Walmart backed up to the railyard.

The tramp hopped out of the dumpster and brushed himself off. He looked dirty in a permanent way, like her cousins in the mine.

Luanne handed him a cig. "Anything good in there?"

He held up a dented can of beans.

Luanne tossed him the lighter and checked her phone again. From the corner of her eye she saw him staring. Luanne knew she made that stupid blue Walmart shirt look better than anyone else. She cocked her hip toward him.

"So, you traveling then?" she asked without looking up.

"Yeh."

Luanne lifted her chin, her eyes still on the phone. "Do you hop trains?"

"Sometimes."

"Where you headed next?"

The tramp nodded down the row of blue cans. "That dumpster there."

She looked up. "No, I mean, where—"

"New Orleans."

Luanne pulled on her cig. "Sometimes I want to get out of here."

The tramp shrugged.

Luanne knew she could have left. Just like her old man. She could barely admit it but whenever she saw trucks pulled off at the rest stops, part of her didn't blame him for leaving.

"You got any food inside," the tramp asked.

"There's a pile of steaks that just expired. I don't know if they're any good."

"Those dates are never right." The tramp chewed on his cigarette.

Luanne laid her cig on the edge of the dumpster. She went inside. Staring at the overflowing shelves, she knew she could make this all disappear. But how could she leave her mom alone? Luanne picked out a few steaks and went back to the tramp who took them into his arm. She stayed close. "Can I take a picture with you?"

The tramp pulled back. "Why?"

"I don't know. I'll think of you." Luanne held out her phone as far as she could and the tramp leaned in awkwardly. When she showed him the picture, he said nothing.

Luanne's mother texted again: *DID YOU GET MY MESSAGE...*

Luanne flicked away her cig and reached for the door. "I've got to get back to work." Without waiting for an answer, she disappeared with a strut, knowing the tramp was still watching.

Inside, Luanne replied: *I GOT IT. I'LL BRING HOME STEAKS.*

WHETHER TO PARTICIPATE OR OBSERVE

A STORY ABOUT CONNECTION

I stood at the edge of the balcony, New Year's Eve at the Fillmore Auditorium, the band on stage behind the iconic crystal chandeliers, music blasting, a huge crowd dancing below.

"I love watching it happen," I told my friend.

"You're a part of it, too, you know?" she said.

Easy to forget with that perfect view. Indeed, I wasn't just watching but in the scene with everyone else. And how often this happens, when we think of ourselves as mere observers, though we're actually participating.

After all, there's a spectrum between participation and observation, always has been, however the line is now confused, wildly contorted by this house of mirrors we call the internet. While our phones encourage us to live vicariously through the lens of others' videos and photos, stewing in a mix of inspiration and envy, I'd like to believe it pushes us toward engagement, toward participation, but I'm pretty sure the opposite is true—a move toward ever more remote observation—and I have a feeling this slant toward observation is making us all miserable.

So what's the alternative, you might ask? More participation.

This makes me think of the anthropologist Bronislaw Malinowski, progenitor of the method of fieldwork aptly named *participant-observation*, who embedded himself with the villagers of the Trobriand Islands for years in the early twentieth century to try and understand their scene. Then he turned around and hollered back to the sedentary armchair theorists in his field, holed up at their universities: Come down off the veranda, come out of your studies and join the people!

Still resonates, yeah? But we're not talking about travelling to some remote island here. We're talking about connecting like we used to, having more conversations face-to-face. It feels daunting: to connect, let alone live the life you really want to live, or to quit your miserable job, to make the art that's burning within, to travel (perhaps to some remote island).

Yet we must. We owe it to ourselves to stop observing and participate, whatever that means to you—but how? We're born to connect with each other, to participate in life together and figure it out. We're not on our own. We've got to trust our instincts.

We need to help each other cross over from observer to participant. You might even say guide one another. This is why we hire business coaches to guide us through our careers. Why we hire therapists to guide us through our heads. Though the truth is we can all be guides.

That friend of mine at the Fillmore was a guide that night, pulling me into the show. And so are you when you call that friend who's having a hard time, or whenever you show up for someone. We ought to give ourselves more credit. We can do this for each other. We should.

Participation is greater than observation. So come off the veranda. Do your thing.

OUT OF LONELINESS
A STORY ABOUT SHARING YOURSELF

You ever heard that joke: no one talks about Jesus' true miracle—having twelve close friends in his 30s. I want to laugh, right, but this one hits uncomfortably close to home.

See my parents still hang out with their high school friends. My grandfather, at ninety-one, still sees his elementary school friends, at least those still around...85 years of friendship! But I have been more, uh, transient in my relationships over the years.

It's not like I've left a trail of burnt bridges. Whenever I see friends from childhood and college and my particularly-roaming twenties, we jump right back in. But nevertheless, I can pretty much count on one hand the number of close friends I have at a given moment.

The difference between my generation of Millennials and those of my parents and grandparents has got to be the pervasive relocation. While they've remained in my hometown their entire lives, I left as soon as I could. My siblings split town, too. Most of my friends from high school left. And nearly everyone I met in college had transplanted from elsewhere. I think it's fair to generalize and call mine a generation of transients.

Calling someone transient is not exactly a compliment. But here we are, untethered from our roots by the promise of a technology making it possible to work from anywhere. "Digital nomad" anyone?

I build houses for a living, so what do I know? It's literally the antithesis of a nomadic life. But I stare at my computer enough to know that it can be a lonely place inside the screen. And while this technology is a relatively recent phenomenon, loneliness is not.

Though the idea of "sharing" has been co-opted by the tech CEOs for their own purposes, I still believe sharing is the cure for loneliness wholesale. A story to illustrate:

I used to live next to this guy who I'll call Alan. His family has lived in the house since the 1940s: first his grandparents, then his parents, and for the last twenty years, him. He's a sweet guy, lifelong bachelor, and regularly poked his head over the fence to show me his winning scratch offs and give an update on the cornhole world championships. I think I might still be his closest friend.

I'm certain Alan has gone days on end without speaking to another person. But his isolation is purely analog. Alan once told me, "I don't have any of that newfangled stuff" (referring to the internet). Yes, he said *newfangled*.

I went into Alan's house every now and then, which is still decorated circa 1972. And every time he wanted to *share*: his photos, his stories, his antique Christmas ornaments. He had a picture of the six-foot diameter willow tree in his backyard from when it was still a sapling, and I couldn't help thinking about John Prine's song Hello In There, when he talks about trees becoming stronger as they grow older, and rivers becoming wilder, but that people mostly become lonesome.

What's John Prine asking of us in his song but to invite a lonely person to share themselves? It's certainly what Alan wanted more than anything. And I actually think his analog ways of connecting are a better answer for curing our digital loneliness than anything the technologists can spit out.

Sharing yourself isn't just about the best parts, the highlights that might go on the socials. That's like screaming into the void. Every time I've done it I come away feeling even more alone than before.

No, the point of sharing yourself is to have it all reflected back at you, so you're reminded of who you are, where you belong, even if it's not perfect. The other day I read that kids who grow up in houses with lots of family photos are better off—because they know where they belong. Someone hitting the "like" button is hardly reaffirming who you are. Much better is talking to real people, friends, looking them in the eyes over a cup of coffee or a plate of lunch.

You ever go into some greasy spoon diner and see a table of old guys sitting around drinking coffee, shooting the shit? *That* is the real-life equivalent to sharing on the internet; but instead of random videos and status updates, it's an imperfect bank of memories getting kicked around, perhaps reshaped, but enjoyed and appreciated nonetheless.

I wish Alan had a crew like that to hang with. It was his birthday last week. 73 years old. I keep the date in my phone so I don't forget to call. We ran back the same old stories and I gave him an update on the kids. He told me about the latest in the world of competitive darts. We shared a small slice of our respective lives and I think we both felt better for it.

In the end, I don't think it's about the amount of friends you have but enjoying the ones right in front of you. And remembering that your very first friend is yourself.

After all, we will spend a lot of time in life alone, but that doesn't mean it has to be lonely.

TOUCH ME

A STORY ABOUT INTIMACY

My wife and I had barely touched each other for six months. Our small house never let us forget it, either, keeping us in close enough proximity to confirm our desire for one another had almost completed its disappearing act.

The marriage was thoroughly sexless by that point, yet it wasn't the sex I missed so much as the lack of any physical contact at all. Trying to salvage the relationship, we saw a couples' therapist who encouraged us to express our desires.

"Touch me," I said.

The next day, sitting at the kitchen table on my laptop, my wife casually leaned on my shoulders and asked what I was working on. The shock of her hands felt so intrusive that I immediately questioned everything I'd asked for.

After twelve years of slowly numbing my desires, I realized I had no idea what I wanted anymore.

We settled on divorce and I found a place of my own. Trying to get out of my head, I dusted off the bike I'd purchased during the pandemic and explored the country roads north of town. One afternoon a buddy joined me, bringing along a woman he'd met online.

She had left a sexless marriage the year before and as we rode side-by-side, I felt a comfort in hearing her stories. Then during a rest break my friend casually asked her: "So, how was that sex party you went to?"

"Oh . . ." She paused. "It was incredible."

For the next ten minutes she detailed the local kink parties she'd been attending. "I didn't realize I was into any of this stuff," she said. "But as you walk around and see the kink, all these different things happening—domination, bondage, orgies—you get these body hits, this intuition of wanting to experience something new."

I noticed my leg bouncing. I'd been telling people for months I wanted to push beyond the edge of my comfort zone. It seemed the moment had arrived.

"Can anyone go to these parties?" I asked.

"If you fill out an application," she said.

That night, with my new condo in darkness, I scrolled through the questions on my phone. Amongst a request for a full-body photo, nude not required, and my thoughts on consent, they asked what I hoped to get from the experience.

I explained my divorce, the wholesale lack of intimacy in my life, an entire preamble to why I was interested. Then I deleted everything and wrote instead: to awaken my desire.

I pushed submit.

A week later, the text came through. My application had been accepted.

Walking up the dimly lit driveway, I entered a sprawling mansion cleared of its furniture in preparation for the hundred-fifty kinksters now arriving. It had also been redecorated.

Two naked women lay on the kitchen island, their bodies adorned with miniature cupcakes; in the corner of the living room, a St. Andrew's cross had been erected for flogging; and beside the stairwell, a trio of costumed bartenders served an assortment of aphrodisiac elixirs.

The host encouraged us to wander the house while the remaining guests showed up.

The rooms had been labeled and outfitted for their evening's purpose. Pillows and candles in the Tantra Room, massage tables in the Erotic Blueprint station, slim mattresses spread throughout the Orgy Dungeon. New arrivals—some in their twenties, some in their seventies, all in varying states of undress—poked their heads in. No touching, we were told, until the opening circle.

The host, a professional dominatrix in a black lace corset, called us to attention where she laid the ground rules. These included: complete sobriety, consent, safe words, and the importance of naming your desires.

"If you desire something," she said, "ask for it with honesty and clear communication. Then accept the answer you receive, whatever it may be."

"Creepiness," she added, "is the refusal to own your desires. So don't be a creep."

To maintain a space where people could explore their desires and find their edge without fear, a team of "desire angels" staffed the party whose job was ensuring guests got the experience they had hoped for. These desire angels made themselves known and one of them, a raven-haired woman with a playful smile, caught my eye from across the room.

With that, the dominatrix cranked the music and declared, "Let's play!"

Within minutes, a woman gripping a leash drug a man on all fours through the crowd. A few feet away, electrified chains zapped a man's bare back. And a woman now tied to the cross began receiving a howler of a flogging.

It had seemed perfectly reasonable, leading up to this moment, to break the spell of a sexless marriage by attending a fully-liberated kink party. Zero to one-hundred, I had joked with friends who knew of my plans. Now, in the middle of it, and flirting with an out-of-body experience, the only word I could muster was overwhelmed.

Unsure what to do, I made a lap through the mansion, watching those better versed in the scene take action—myself stuck as an observer, unable to engage.

Perhaps noticing my uncertainty, a blonde desire angel in white lingerie appeared by my side.

"How are you doing?" she asked.

"I'm not sure," I said.

"Tell me your desires?"

"I don't know."

She looked into my eyes. "Breathe into your cock. What does it tell you?"

I tried breathing into my cock. It wasn't speaking.

"Come with me." She took my hand, guiding me to the Tantra room where calm music played and a few others cuddled amongst the pillows and candles. She sat me down in an oversized chair. "I want to get you out of your head and into your body."

She asked again for my desires.

"I think I'd like to touch you," I said.

"Good," she said. "You can touch me anywhere except my genitals, and no kissing. These are my boundaries. Now, be quiet and let me worship you."

She mounted the chair and for ten minutes whispered all kinds of sweet nothings into my ear. The noise in my head seemed to quiet down. When she finished, I thanked her and said I was ready to get back out there.

Knowing everyone at this party was a potential lover, though, inverted the monogamous mindset I'd lived for years. I still couldn't bring myself to ask anyone for anything.

Am I broken? I asked myself, descending into the orgy dungeon.

Two dozen partygoers filled the mattresses in a tangle of flesh, legs in the air, heads bobbing, guttural noises punctuating the house music. I voyeured for a minute, feeling no closer to understanding my desires, and then noticed a small nook in the room where another desire angel sat beside a floor lamp.

"But how do you know if it's desire you're feeling?" I asked her. "What if it's something else?"

"Imagine a time you were completely excited. Embody that," she said. "That's the feeling of desire." I closed my eyes, manifesting the feeling.

"Now, try the opposite. Embody the feeling of repulsion," she continued. "These are the ends of the spectrum. Everything you feel moves one way or the other. You need to tap into this to know which way you're going."

As I tapped in, a man began screaming behind me at regular intervals. My curiosity turned me around where I found him, nearly-naked, on his knees, one woman whipping him and another squeezing his testicles. The women and I exchanged glances.

I might not know what I want, I thought, but I don't think I want that.

They had used a phrase at the opening circle: don't yuck my yum. Despite not understanding my own desires, I sought comfort in not judging others as they explored theirs and resigned myself to not figuring out anything that night.

Then I went into the one room I hadn't yet visited: the Erotic Blueprint. I'd heard earlier from the man wielding the flog that this was a must.

The Erotic Blueprint is like the five love languages for arousal, the way we are uniquely turned on as individuals.

I lay on a massage table in my underwear and for the next ten minutes, as the practitioner explained, he would do a series of two touches, asking which of them I preferred. Some touches were light, some firm. Some with silk, some with pointed implements. I got whipped a few times. Regular A/B testing.

I soon learned that I have an energetic and sensual arousal pattern, meaning it's the anticipation of intimacy that turns me on most of all. The taboo nature of kink is an arousal pattern in itself, the lowest on my list, which explained in part why I hadn't been drawn into much of the party.

Desire was in me, I realized. It simply hadn't been called out.

I would have been satisfied if the party had ended then. But with half an hour left, I returned to the Tantra room. As far as energy was concerned, this space had the mellow kind I wanted. I sat against the wall, breathing, taking it in.

Then the door to the room opened and the raven-haired desire angel I'd noticed at the beginning of the night walked in. She came straight over and asked if she could join me. I said yes and, now side-by-side, she asked the question of the night once more. "What are your desires?"

I thought for a moment: considering what I'd seen tonight at the party, the edge of my comfort zone long gone in the rearview, my broken marriage, my new life at hand. Then I stopped thinking.

I looked at this woman, earnestly asking what I wanted, waiting to have a real conversation about desire. And for the first time that night, I actually felt it.

"Touch me," I said.

GETTING DIVORCED
A STORY ABOUT PARTING WAYS

A month before the wedding, I went into the mountains behind our house to gather aspen trees for which I'd use to build a chuppah for our ceremony. As tradition goes, the chuppah is a symbol of the home my wife and I would build together as a married couple—seeing as this is such a beautiful notion, and that I had built the thing to last, after the ceremony we brought it to our house, sticking it in the corner of the yard.

We placed a little table underneath the chuppah where we intended to spend mornings sipping coffee, drinking wine in the evenings, and taking time to appreciate the life we'd built together, though it never really happened. Mostly, the little table got in the way when I cut the grass.

A couple years passed before the wind knocked the chuppah over, splitting one of the upper boughs in two. I didn't think much of it, propping the whole thing back up without making repairs. *Still standing*, I figured. Eventually, of course, that attitude would split a lot more than a piece of wood.

\ \ \

Four months ago my wife and I decided to separate. She came into the room after putting the kids to bed. "We need to be honest with each other," she began. Something had brought it all to a head that evening. Earlier in the day, I had been looking up *how to know if you should get divorced*. We'd both reached the same decision, separately, together.

It was one of the calmest conversations we'd ever had, perhaps the best in years: for once we weren't hiding from each other, ignoring the dissatisfaction swelling beneath our marriage. And the odd part in making the call was that it wasn't hard at all. Thirty minutes in we poured some whiskey, moved to the couch, and even laughed once as we reviewed how we'd ended up here.

For all the ease of honesty that night before, though, we hadn't deluded ourselves into thinking it would be easy. In a way this wasn't new to us at all—we'd called off our original wedding three weeks out, broke up, then got back together, seeing it through six months later. We knew something about how hard parting ways could be—but seeing our two young boys in the morning qualified that in the heaviest way and I couldn't keep it together when they gave me a hug as I left for work. I shuffled around that day like I was in a dream, lost somewhere in the surrealism of a world still sleeping on this new reality I had to face. Yet it was as real as could be.

While we used the word *separate*, there wasn't much question of us working it out—I guess *divorce* still sounded a little too harsh—because it had been years since either of us could honestly say we were happy. On paper, it looked pretty good, sure, but once you start going through the motions in life it's easy to gloss over the deficiencies, the discomforts, the disillusions, until soon enough your "must haves" turn into "nice to haves" and you realize you've both willingly compromised yourselves to the lowest common denominator.

It should be obvious where a reductive trajectory eventually leads, even while certain visions of the future are achieved. We had a house, a small piece of land, and more important than anything, our kids. Beyond that, we still like each other. There was no abuse, addiction, or infidelity, but along with the absence of these came the absence of love, at least anything resembling romance. Simply put: we'd always been better friends than lovers. Nothing had changed.

We started telling people, slowly widening the circle, but notably saving the news from our parents. Maybe it was guilt that held us back, maybe shame, or maybe that telling them had a certain finality to which we hadn't yet worked up. When we finally did I was met with the kind of unconditional love and support that makes me lucky to have the family I do, along with the opportunity to take another look at what I'd seen of divorce growing up.

Though I knew a lot of kids whose parents were divorced, only one of them had parents who were still friends. That seemed awfully strange; bitterness seemed the norm. Remembering this has helped us understand how exactly we want to shape ours.

The best thing that anyone has said throughout this whole ordeal is that we can make it look however we want it to look. One prescient vision stands out from last year, long before this decision was made, when our seven-year-old son told me his friend had parents who don't like each other anymore. That was the language he had to describe divorce. So when we told the boys, we made a point to provide new words: that we love each other as friends, we just don't want to be married anymore.

\ \ \

A week after our first conversation about splitting up, a full windstorm came through and blew the chuppah over, cracking the whole thing in half. Poetic, right? The next day I dismantled it altogether, backing out screws I remembered driving in years before, and stacked the pieces against the fence, not sure what to do with the wood but not interested in looking at this broken idea of our marriage any longer.

Over the last few years I've come to think most decisions in life are made around comfort. And it's more motivating to move away from discomfort rather than towards greater comfort, assuming you're already pretty comfortable. Things were plenty comfortable for us, whereby some have wondered aloud: isn't that enough? But no, it's not.

My wife and I have since talked about the complacency and resignation in our marriage as limiting. And when you limit yourself in one area of life, especially in a partnership, you limit your life wholesale. For us, in many ways, this decision is about removing these self-imposed limitations. In our case, that means divorce—though I don't necessarily think it has to come to that.

I'm amazed by the kinds of honest conversations I've had with my friends since sharing this news. The other day one of them said: you sharing all of this makes me want to tell you about the insecurities I have about my marriage. And so he did, and I've never felt closer to him for it. It seems like it often takes tragedy—miscarriage, cancer, infidelity, divorce—for people to open up. Why don't we just talk about this shit instead of hiding behind a veneer of perfection? I'm guilty as anyone, to be sure, but there's no question it'd do us all a lot of good.

The poet Charles Bukowski once wrote in his novel *Women*: "Pain arrives, BANG, and there it is. It sits on you. It's real. And to anybody watching, you look foolish. Like you've suddenly become an idiot. There's no cure for it unless you know somebody who understands how you feel, and knows how to help."

Interestingly, my wife and I have been that for each other. It's odd to find both cause for and comfort from suffering in the same person, but sometimes nobody else can understand what it feels like to be in a certain moment, so you lean in all the same. Both our therapist and mediator have said we're good at divorce. That's not the accolade we were going for at the outset, but I think it speaks to the mutual respect we're trying to hold onto. Mainly, that we understand we're forever connected by our children, and beyond this, we have a longstanding friendship currently being exhumed from beneath the ashes of this marriage, so for the sake of not only the present but the future, that mutual respect feels like everything.

Nevertheless, we're also on our own.

\ \ \

About six weeks ago I moved out of the house and into a condo, which I've slowly been making a place both settled and exciting for myself and the boys when they're with me.

When you have kids, sometimes you yearn for the unencumbered nature of life before children, sometimes you simply dream of quiet. Then you get it and it's almost unbearable. The silence is deafening. I haven't been drinking very much lately, but the first night in the condo I needed something to take the edge off so I grabbed the tequila and poured it in the only vessel I had, my grandmother's teacup. I sat on my bare mattress, my back against the wall, not sure if I should laugh or cry, so I did a bit of both.

The quiet hits me in the weirdest of ways. Drips of syrup still on the table from breakfast while I'm eating dinner by myself. A loose sock on the floorboard of my truck. Messes I'd prefer to leave as proof of life as a father.

And, then again, it's also nice to get a reprieve from the relentlessness of modern parenthood. I actually have time for myself in way that I can enjoy, without feeling guilty for not being present with my kids when I've got other things to do. A friend of mine who's also divorced said maybe this is how raising kids is supposed to look—not the divorce, but the regular breaks that let you renew yourself so you can truly show up for those who need you.

I won't deny this has been hard on us as a family. Hard on the kids who show it in their behavior, and all my wife and I can do is hold the space for them to feel it. But I remind myself of two things:

1. When I told my best friend that we're going to be okay, he said, "No, you need to adjust your language. You're going to be better." And that's the honest truth.
2. I've talked to too many people who have said, "Yeah, my parents are still together, but they should have gotten divorced a long time ago."

I'd never want our kids saying that about us. Bitterness hadn't yet crept into our marriage, but if we had stayed together I'm sure it would have.

So even though the marriage itself didn't last, I don't see this as a failed relationship. Rather I see it as one that's been fulfilled. My wife used a beautiful phrase to describe what we had: *soul contract*. And our soul contract was to bring our two boys into this world. For any uncertainties I might've held about our relationship, I never had any doubts about that. And now, with that purpose fulfilled, it's time for both of us to find out what's next—as we continue to raise our children as coparents, while freeing each other to find other purposes that could not be supported in this relationship.

\ \ \

Obviously, I can't distill eight years of marriage into two-thousand words. But I'll sum it up like this: the other day I was back at the old house, grabbing a few things, taking my time, hanging out. At one point, looking for the kids, I went outside and found them by the fence, building a fort with the wood from the broken chuppah. I don't want to put too neat of a bow on this, but there's something to be said for our children still finding shelter in the dismantled pieces of our marriage.

As much as I want to say everything happens for a reason, maybe it's just that time marches on—and if you're still around, still living, what else is there to do but look back on all of it and say, we're still here—which might be reason enough.

I WILL BE A PRETTY THING

A SHORT STORY

In two weeks, their family and friends would be sitting in the pews, the adults waiting patiently like adults, the children fidgeting like children, and the man would be standing in the noiseless chapel thumbing the rings in his pocket.

His mind would be scouring the days, hoping for some kind of answer, until he remembered today—this day now outside at the café—when he asked if she loved him.

The woman moved her spoon an inch, then her knife, tidying up. "Don't turn my words," she said. "I called it *old-fashioned*. And I still don't know why it matters?"

The woman's face looked pale in the sun. It distracted him. "This has always been our plan," he said. "This is what we want."

The waiter came across the patio with a fresh bottle of beer for the man. The man lowered his voice to a hoarse whisper. "People are counting on us."

The woman didn't change her voice at all. "People want what's best for us. They will understand."

The waiter started pouring the beer but the man waved him off. He stared at his family ring on the woman's finger, upside down, digging into the tablecloth. "It's too late," he said.

The highway sound droned through the tables as the man poured the rest of his beer, fast, sending foam over the rim. The woman watched the foam wet the table and that the man hadn't noticed.

"I know it's too late," the woman said. She picked her iced tea up and held it at her lips. "It's too late for anything."

A breeze blew and the man imagined goosebumps on her and he went to the car for a jacket. In all this sun it had never occurred to him to that she might get cold.

SLOW DOWN

MEDITATING WITH GRAPEFRUITS
A STORY ABOUT FEELING IT

I like the idea of meditating but have no fucking idea what I'm doing when I try, so mostly, I don't. But I think I've figured out something approximate with grapefruits. Allow me to explain.

This began in Patagonia fifteen years ago as I camped outside of a little Argentine village called El Chaltén and ate a grapefruit on the banks of a meandering river. After living out of a backpack for a month, I'd been savoring every bite of food I carried. But this grapefruit was different. I vividly remember peeling it to the sounds of the rippling water, portioning out each section, slowly eating them, taking in all of their sour flavor.

Of course, I'd eaten grapefruits before. Growing up, my mom would cut them in half for breakfast and we'd pour way too much sugar on top, scooping out the insides with sharp-edged spoons, slurping down the sugar juice left in the bowl—but sitting by that river was the first time I'd eaten one without trying to mask the true taste of the fruit. And this is how I inadvertently discovered my path to meditation.

By now it has become somewhat of a ritual. Taking five minutes to pay attention to what's in front of me, letting the grapefruit do the work of boxing out any judgement. I guess you'd call it my stand in for a mantra.

Because I find it hard not to judge my feelings when they arise. For a long time when a thought came up which I didn't like I pushed it off altogether, hoping it would disappear if buried deep enough. But, no, that's not how it works—for those thoughts there's only one way out and it's right between the eyes. Anything shoved into the bottom of our souls only rots and festers until it hollows us out completely, or else eats its way out sideways in the nastiest manner imaginable. Depression, anxiety, cancer . . . nasty.

I know because I've been there. Waking up every morning with a pit in my stomach at the thought of facing another day. Not wanting to be who I was. That shit lasted for years. And the worst part was I felt entirely alone in my feelings, like no one could possibly understand what I was going through.

Alongside a few years of therapy, it only took about 80,000 people to finally change my mind.

Bonnaroo music festival, 2006. Late nights wandering through the fields of central Tennessee, beams of light flying from tents where bands played and the intrinsic glow of each person there to enjoy it. Cynics might pin it on something else, but how can you not have an altered state of mind with that many people in the same place for the same reason.

The strangers I ran into felt like brothers and sisters, and somehow I knew they felt the same exact way. There was an overwhelming sense of connection among us all. Durkheim might refer to this as our collective effervescence. Emerson would say it is the over-soul: "The universal beauty to which every part and particle is equally related." Whatever it's called, I was no longer alone.

But that's what art is for, isn't it? Feeling things we might not be able to feel on our own. Why 80,000 people can feel connected at a music festival. Why you might start crying watching a movie or with a novel in your hand. In the end, what is life itself but art!

If you don't believe it, maybe you don't live your life with enough style. Read this from Charles Bukowski:

> *Style is the answer to everything.*
> *A fresh way to approach a dull or dangerous thing.*
> *To do a dull thing with style is preferable to doing a dangerous thing*
> *without it.*
> *To do a dangerous thing with style is what I call art.*

If you want your life to be art, you've got to live dangerously. This does not mean taking unnecessary risks and acting like a fool. No, it simply means feeling everything to the fullest—the good, the bad, and all that lies between—welcoming it inside, then letting it out right between your eyes. As it turns out *that* is meditation.

To be fair, though, sometimes this is asking a lot. I'm still working on it myself. I don't expect that will ever stop. And whenever this stuff starts feeling like too much, I try and forget about it altogether—instead I go eat a grapefruit.

IN THE THICK OF IT
A STORY ABOUT PRESENCE

I don't write about my kids very often. Mainly because I write after they've gone to bed, and during that time of quiet respite I like escaping to another headspace. But with parenthood always humming in the back of my mind, it's ultimately inescapable, influencing just about everything I do. Thankfully, much of what I've picked up being a father applies far beyond raising kids.

Number one on the list: presence.

The other day I was sitting on the couch, messing around on my phone. My four-year-old wanted to play. I'm sure I muttered some answer. So, the boy jumped on me and, in one swift and surprisingly graceful motion, kicked me in the nuts, pulled my hair, and head butted me in the face.

Sometimes it's nice to have a violent reminder to get your head in the game. Kids have their ways of willing the presence out of you—and they often get it, whether you're looking to provide or not. If only other pursuits employed such assertive methods.

This writing gig, for one, requires presence two times over: presence during the act of actually putting words on the page and also presence throughout the day, noticing details, how people walk and talk with each other, how the light changes across the street in the afternoons, how it feels to be in a marriage, and all of the other things you must put into a story to make it feel *real.*

But in this world, there are armies of ulterior motives fighting for our presence, undermining our efforts to put that energy toward pursuits which lack that alluring sense of instant gratification, but which would be more meaningful in the long run (e.g. relationships, experiences, making art, etc. etc. etc.).

In his book *Calypso*, David Sedaris describes what it's like to host his friends with young children, and how completely violated he feels by the time they leave. David Sedaris, it should be noted, has no children. I do—and I often feel the same way.

But perhaps a bit of violation is necessary. If it's against the sanctity of our ability to stray off course, procrastinate, and generally fuck off when we'd be better off paying attention, then I'd say that violation is warranted. If I'm sleeping through life, I'll take some cold water to the face.

Because a lack of presence doesn't just drop you at a neutral baseline.

My temper, for instance, is directly correlated with my presence. If I'm preoccupied, my mind elsewhere, thinking about something that ought to be done, my patience gets thin—I notice it with the kids—but when my mind is quiet, I can play for hours without thinking about being anywhere else.

Of course, focusing on presence is easier said than done. You wouldn't have yoga and meditation if it were. But in this time of *always on*, with emails and texts arriving at all times, and the increasingly dissolved boundaries between business and pleasure, it seems harder than ever to eliminate the distractions.

This goes for both those with and without kids. We're all dealing with plenty of life—and life is hard however you slice it. As Mark Manson points out it in his book *The Subtle Art of Not Giving A F*ck*, no one is free of problems, they just differ depending on your circumstances. Single people deal with one set of challenges, married people another, and the same is true of rich versus poor.

As a political science professor of mine liked to say: "Choose your solutions, choose your problems."

I think it's fair to say that our modern culture is exacerbating these issues, wholesale, regardless of our specific problems. Since I have willingly chosen parenthood problems, I would like to share two recently learned facts:

1. The majority of states have laws saying puppies must not be separated from their mothers before eight weeks of age.
2. Daycare centers licensed for infants will take children as young as six weeks.

Take that information at face value, but I'll tell you how I interpret it: we live in a society that recognizes the importance of keeping puppies with their mothers, but doesn't afford that same respect to its own citizens. Exemplifying, in one specific way, how our society is generally set up for anti-presence.

Things pull at our attention from every direction. Utter distraction. A phone constantly buzzing in our pockets. Newer, better, faster products we *must* purchase. A hundred alternate lifestyles we could be living: minimalist, maximalist, digitally nomadic. And, of course, making money to finance all of it.

A distracted mind is advantageous to many interests, with the notable exception of our own self-interest. Because attention is a zero-sum game— as we dilute our attention with distraction, hardly any is left for the present moment.

Ram Dass, the famed spiritual philosopher, once commanded: BE HERE NOW. It's a simple task. But like most simple things, pulling it off is a tall order. So, here's to this moment, right now (and it headbutting you into the present, metaphorically speaking).

WHEN YOU'RE THE SUCKER
A STORY ABOUT TRUST

As a freshman in college, back in 2005, I had some car trouble—so I brought it in, gave the deskman the run down, and signed off on $350 of service before the mechanic even had a look. As a fresh-faced student, buzzed on my newfound independence, this seemed normal. Until, that is, I told my father who said: "Tell them to stop work immediately and give you a proper quote."

Not only did the auto shop refuse to stop work but they insisted I pay in cash—apparently, I decided, they had done this before—and I quickly realized they had taken me for a sucker. And they were right.

My father said don't worry, it happens to everyone, which didn't really ease the pain at the time but it's certainly true. You've got to be the sucker a few times, and with each instance you get more motivation not to be one again.

Still, the question remains: how to avoid being the sucker? Well, I've come to think it's all about understanding trust.

After the fact, an older and wiser friend told me: two people you've got to trust in life are your doctor and mechanic. They know things you don't, which puts them in a position of authority—authority of knowledge—and if you don't trust them, you could easily be taken advantage of.

In the context of medicine and/or car maintenance, there are certain barriers that hopefully weed out the hustlers and scammers, con men and grifters (i.e. med school, online reviews). This is all fine and good for the relatively infrequent visits to these fields of practice. If only the same could be said for the omnipresent arena in which we all play these days: the internet.

Ah, the internet. In this place, trust is not so readily apparent. It's weird how trusting we are inside the internet. All it takes is a blue check mark and, worthy or not, people suddenly have the credibility of a standup citizen. Or better yet a "company" that exists only because it has a social profile.

I am thinking specifically of Instagram, particularly the things being sold there. The advertisements just keep coming, hit after hit, slowly convincing you that your jaw is flabby and you need to chew a rubber ball to tone it up. Did I purchase this jaw exercise ball—yes, I did—and along with the rest every single time I've bought something off Instagram, I've regretted it.

To date, I have procured the following Insta-purchases:

1. A colorful, short sleeve button down shirt
2. A kaleidoscope
3. A fleece jacket
4. The jaw exercise thing

For some reason, I've waited until after I've input my cc information to look up the product and see if it's a scam. What I've found it that most of these "brands" are simple pass-thru entities that resell items from Ali Baba. Then shipping takes three weeks on the literal slow boat and what shows up is a marred bag and a major discrepancy between the well-done photos and the item itself. I should probably keep these past purchases in a little box to remind me that not all that glitters is gold.

There's that saying: If you don't know who the sucker in the room is, it's probably you. Despite the cynicism of the idea, it's cliché for a reason. Not everyone in the world is that nice. And on that note, there's one other concept I want to bring into the conversation before wrapping this up: karma.

Karma makes you feel better about being the sucker. When my bike got stolen in college a few years later, the only relief came in knowing that bad karma awaited the thief. I'm not sure if you yourself gather bad karma for enjoying a little schadenfreude against the perpetrators—this seems like the cosmic equivalent of double dipping—but, definitely, you gain no karmic credit from being the victim.

Being a sucker is simply collateral damage to karma working. So, in turn, we must refine our trust, keep faith that most people are good-hearted, and try our best not to be the sucker out there. That's all we can really do. In the meantime, karma keeps doing its thing.

The one thing I will say for sure is that the auto shop which scammed me all those years ago has now been demolished and some new apartments stand in its place. I guess you call that progress.

EAT A PEACH
A STORY ABOUT SEASONS

Late summer in Colorado is all about the peaches—Palisade peaches—grown on the Western Slope, the desert side of the state, and they are hands down the most delicious peaches you'll ever taste (sorry, Georgia). For two months they show up at farmers' markets, street corner pop-up tents, and throughout the grocery. Then they're gone ... until next year.

The other day, scrolling through the socials, I saw the late Anthony Bourdain lamenting the way we eat—the way we walk into a grocery expecting to find anything we want, whenever we want, completely disassociated from whatever might be in season—the fluorescent lights of the modern supermarket shining on a society unbound by the seasons.

I'm going to reiterate Bourdain here: this is a bad thing.

Just because you *can* do something out of time doesn't mean you *should*. And the bland hard peaches you buy at the grocery in January will never make the grade. But this isn't just about the practical costs, like shipping produce up from Chile when they're hot and we're not, because the philosophical toll might even be greater: trading natural rhythms for artificial consistency, and a mediocre consistency at that.

There is much to be said for the ebb and flow of all things. Seasons of want, seasons of plenty—where the highs make you appreciate the lows, and the lows allow you to fully experience the highs. As Kahlil Gibran wrote in *The Prophet*: "The deeper that sorrow carves into your being, the more joy you can contain." A level-best coasting doesn't quite have the same effect.

But before we get too solemn here, let's return to peaches: there is great anticipation here in Colorado for the ripening every summer. And when the fruit finally comes, people indulge—maybe even gorge—in the abundance. Peaches every way: grilled, baked, added to pastries and pies, or eaten whole. Then, to keep the vibe going, you can jar them and get that taste of summer all winter long.

Let's talk about that homesteader preservation. It's a bit like storing memories, isn't it?

Canned, jarred, and flash-frozen "at the peak of freshness"... these are pretty remarkable methods of keeping food. A kind of snapshot taking us back to whatever season the fruit or vegetable came from, more or less (not really counting limp green beans here).

While nothing will beat picking a cherry tomato off the vine and popping it right into your mouth, a really good tomato sauce might perk the tastebuds just enough to take you back to summer, if only for a moment. Seasons might be ever-changing, but no one said you can't make occasional off-peak return visits.

Of course, not everyone can or will grow their own food. No doubt, the discussion of access to fresh produce and the blight of food deserts in this country is a much bigger, deeper, and more complex topic—but, suffice it to say that "from a can" is indeed where many, if not most, people get their peaches.

Am I referring to that classic song of my youth, regarding the reality of our fruit-related expectations, by The Presidents of the United States of America? Yes, I am.

Once this current peach season is over, I'll be eating them from a can, too—but for now I'm going to indulge until every ripe peach has disappeared.

FINDING THE ENERGY
A STORY ABOUT TIME

As a custom homebuilder, I talk about wood more than the average guy. If it's not *this* species versus *that* species, it's the minutiae of different grain types, the natural figuring and movement, whether it imparts more of a modern or traditional aesthetic—I could go on here but I won't, because lost in those nuances, it's easy (as they say) to miss the forest for the trees.

Being consumed by the details of wood is to gloss over the fact that we're discussing years of life visibly condensed into a single object. With those tree rings making up the grain, you have a literal record of the seasons, the droughts and the deluges, the good times and bad, a history of life so accurate that scientists have developed the field of dendrochronology using solely tree rings to recreate Earth's past.

It's worth pausing here to revisit a law from Physics 101: energy can neither be created nor destroyed, only converted from one form to another.

I've never been very good at the hard sciences—you're looking at a degree in anthropology, right here—but this begs the question: what happens to all the energy that went into growing the tree once it dies? If there are 30, 50, 100+ years stored inside those tree rings, where does it go in the end?

Considering it's the sun which powers the growth of a tree, it seems to me there are two natural paths for this energy: 1) the long decay . . . rotting, or 2) the nuclear reaction . . . fire.

I think about the latter every time I throw a log onto a campfire—the years of sunshine being released at once—and maybe that's why you can stare at a fire for hours without getting bored. Hard to ignore all those sunny days going back into the atmosphere.

But this isn't about physics. It's about humans. So while the sun drives the growth of trees and life in general, there's another force of nature, equally universal, which provides for our growth as individuals—*time*.

We harness time like leaves harness light, using time itself to build our relationships, our expertise, to craft our life into something of meaning. In the same way tree rings reveal years of growth, so do the layers of experience piled onto the things we value. And just like the energy of the sun, the time is stored there in our knowledge, waiting to be released.

Unlike the trees, of course, we have the free will to choose when and where our time energy is both collected and dispensed. Meaning we can always redirect our time toward something else if and when we see fit.

I balk at the line: *I don't have enough time.* We've all got the same amount of time; some of us are simply more honest than others in how we choose to spend it. Barring circumstances of hardship, this is about priorities. And saying "I don't have enough time" is just a disingenuous way of saying "I'd rather spend my time elsewhere."

It may be cliché, but in the end, the greatest gift we can give anyone, including ourselves, is our time. What interests me, though, is not the way we must spend 10,000 hours practicing a skill to become a master, a la Malcolm Gladwell, but how we collect our time for the most meaningful and reactive release.

Certainly, some phones-down, undivided attention with a friend over lunch is time well-spent. But it's also ephemeral, and I think there's something to be said for gathering time into a single, tangible offering: a handwritten letter, something you've made, and the more time it takes, the better.

A handwritten letter means more than a text or an email exactly because it takes more time to produce it. And on the backend, the effect of receiving such a thing lasts a whole lot longer. This must strike somewhere in the subconscious, almost beyond description, because we can sense the difference between something done on the cheap versus something done with care.

I have a friend who makes custom furniture and though we could talk about the reasons his craftsmanship and quality are far superior to something that arrives packed down in a box, I think you actually *feel* it when you sit down in one of his handmade chairs. It radiates the time that went into crafting it. Mass production can never check that box. And in the case of such a wooden chair, you might feel the warmth of that sunshine, too.

Here's to time well spent.

A BUNGALOW
IN AUSTIN, TX

A SHORT STORY

Bernadette smiled through her screen door. The high-rise across Rainey
street finally got its windows.

Over the sixty years Bernadette had lived there, her little bungalow had
settled into the earth, leaning a few degrees north, but so gently had it
happened as she'd come and gone each day that she only noticed it now,
admiring the reflection of her slanted home in the perfectly plumb grid
of new glass.

She patted her chipped door frame and shuffled down to the street, step-
ping over construction debris, avoiding the gutted houses lining the block.

No, Bernadette would never forget the April when her neighbors all sold
out to the developers. Nor would she would believe it when the warm

living rooms where they'd played cards on Saturday nights became the hippest bars in the city, or so those neighbors liked to brag.

"Fools," she chided.

At the end of the street, things felt like they used to. Overgrown, untouched, left alone. Bernadette slipped through a tunnel in the button-bush and followed a worn path to the river.

Humming some Patsy Cline, she unlaced her dusty boots and walked barefoot to the water's edge. Bernadette pulled half a crusty baguette from her pocket and tossed it in. "At least you're still here," she said as the old red-eared slider floated to the surface.

The turtle gulped at the bread as the sound of a jackhammer puttered over the languid river and Bernadette took a long and easy breath, unbuttoning the top of her blouse, letting the late autumn sun shine on her chest.

FEROCIOUS TRANQUILITY

A STORY ABOUT INNER PEACE

We don't deserve anything in life. Harsh, right? But I say this with a whole-hearted belief in humanity—in human rights, in community, in the beauty of thinking not *me* but *we*—and yet, I also believe that none of the privileges we enjoy can be taken for granted.

If we didn't have to fight for them ourselves, someone else did. All the things we patriotically refer to as a *right*, began as a fight. Nothing worthwhile gets handed over freely, except, perhaps, life itself. And so be it. Without struggle, the spoils of victory cannot be appreciated.

You can apply this to anything—and we should— but as it often goes when the world feels out of our control, especially in these modern times, I think we've got to first turn inward, putting the ideas to work on ourselves. Because if we want tranquility in the world, we need to start by finding the tranquility within.

Thich Nhat Hanh, the Buddhist philosopher, explains in his book *How to Fight* that looking after your own well-being is inseparable from looking after others.

A book on fighting from a Buddhist monk might sound contradictory, but it's a study in contrasts, the opposition of two halves, at odds with one another and yet harmonious. To achieve peace of mind, we've got to fight for it—the tiger sleeps well because she is ferocious.

Like it or not, we're in a battle every day, fending off assailants from all sides. It's not an attack in the traditional sense. The enemies aren't obvious. In fact, they usually want us to be their friends. Convenience, social media, the endless hustle—they're out there desperately trying to convince us we need them, that sacrificing our peace of mind for their sake is worth it.

Did you ever see that show on History Channel called *Life After People*? It hypothesized what might happen if we disappeared. How the plants and animals would move into the vacant cities, reclaiming them as their own—during the Covid lockdown, we saw just that—because if you ever let down your guard, you'll find that all life is fighting its own battle and will gladly take up residence in your absence.

Of course, that doesn't only apply to physical space. When we're mentally checked out, that real estate is just as valuable. The mind predators are on the prowl, as well, waiting to pounce. Take this idea from another great Eastern philosopher, Jiddu Krishnamurti, who said the mind is like soil. If we give our problems too much attention, they grow like weeds. If we ignore them, they wither.

I suppose much of this comes down to perspective, the context we place upon the things we see. As they say, perception is reality. And there is tranquility around us every day that can be appreciated, if approached right.

It's easy to imagine the tranquility of sitting beside a mountain stream, listening to it ripple through the shade; but what if the same could be said for water running through the gutter beside a city street? Once you get close enough, is there any difference? Water carries with it peacefulness no matter the environment, if you only choose to see it. The same can be said for ferocity, too.

Not long ago, a flooring contractor and I were discussing the certain tranquility of looking at such a river, a campfire, how you can watch these things seemingly forever—and he added one more item to the list: a craftsman at work. Imagine it: a carpenter, a chef, a computer programmer . . . the sounds of the saw, the knife, the keyboard, the focus in their eyes, the finished product slowly coming to life on a wall, a plate, the screen. The tranquility is in there, as well, especially when coupled with intensity. Maybe you'd call that flow.

There are things we all must do to survive this world—work being one among many—but to find that peace of mind, remember where to put the fight.

A CASE FOR WRITING THINGS DOWN
A STORY ABOUT OBSERVATION

For maybe twelve years now, I've carried a notebook in my back left pocket. Along with my wallet, phone, and keys, it's become part of the essentials. Because it keeps my mind straight.

A lot of mundane things go into the notebook: grocery lists, to dos, people I ought to catch up with. But, on occasion, I write down a thought that's worth something. I'm talking about observations, fragments of memories, interesting facts—which, for reasons both known and unknown, seem notable.

A couple of recent notes:

1. Weeds are survivors, the hardiest of plants, something to admire if you look at them right
2. If someone is too important, too celebrated, put them in a group of plural—pluralize them (i.e. the kings of England, the actors of Hollywood, etc.). They immediately seem less important.

As a storyteller, these little things can make the difference between getting called for bullshit and writing something that feels real. In his poem, *my friend william*, Charles Bukowski says, "his garden is a paradise / the heels of his shoes are always level / and his handshake is firm"—that middle line blows me away. It tells you everything about this man.

More importantly, and universally, writing these things down forces me to pay attention and keeps me from gliding mindlessly through life.

To be sure, I fuck around on my phone plenty, especially when I've got a few minutes to kill. However, I love sitting in a coffee shop, for instance, listening to the sounds around me. The conversations . . . people say the craziest shit in public. When most people stare at their phone all of the time, I guess it's easy to assume no one is listening. I've gotten great restaurant recommendations this way. A couple of new jokes. And, as far as figuring out how to write dialogue, it's gold.

Carrying a notebook generally coincides with when I started taking writing seriously. However, I'd argue that both the notebook habit and the writing followed a personal revival in observation.

A quick but relevant sidebar: around thirteen I got incredibly self-conscious about fitting in with my friends—wearing the clothes, getting the haircut, saying the right things—and so I spent a lot of time watching what everyone else was doing. As anxiety-ridden as I was back then, I wouldn't trade the experience for anything because it was my first effort at serious observation. And the self-awareness I have now is a direct result of the self-consciousness I felt back then. In fact, I've come to believe you cannot be self-aware without having been self-conscious first.

But observation . . . the notebook turns it into a treat. Alongside ambitious meal planning, I want to fill the page with the things I see and hear and feel. It might sound a little sanctimonious, but the notebook does a lot to keep me present. (I should also admit that I often write notes in my phone. I like the way they synch to the computer.)

One final thing: writing thoughts down frees up mental space. This goes for snapshot takes in a pocket notebook to the deep confessions of a diary. I'm not a great journaler, but when I'm trying to sort out what's going on in my head there's something cathartic about putting it on the page. And even when I can't figure it out, which is mostly the case, the effect remains because whatever it was is not in your mind anymore.

There was a time I was afraid of what I might put on the page if I was being honest. And then I realized the scarier the thought, the more important it usually is. Once it's on the paper, you can do whatever you want with it. Save it, recycle it, burn it. You have effectively donated those thoughts to another place and time. Getting it out there, that's the win.

To bring it on home, observing the world is worthwhile but observing yourself is worth everything. Do it. Then write it down.

ONE FOR
THE MAILMAN
A STORY ABOUT LETTERS

When I was growing up our mailman, Nick, was a local hero. While on his route he once saw a little girl fall through the ice on a neighborhood pond and saved her life. He showed me the laminated newspaper article and I still remember the black-and-white photo of him standing beside his mail truck, humbly beaming at the good deed.

Saving lives is the epitome of heroic, no doubt, but I want to suggest that all mailmen and mailwomen are heroes in their own right, if perhaps with a lowercase *h*, and by that I mean they single-handedly carry on an ancient tradition: sending letters.

In these times of emails and texts and push notifications, hell, even phone calls, the handwritten letter stands alone. It remains the most intimate, most sincere way we can communicate short of having a face-to-face conversation—and, even then, we might write something in a letter long before we're prepared to say it out loud.

There is nothing like getting a handwritten letter. It is raw and wild: unruly handwriting, misspelled words, poor grammar, and yet that is exactly the beauty of it. You can actually *feel* another person in that ink. It's the rare medium which compliments the communication, rather than diminishes it.

I've long thought that handwritten words are the closest we get to seeing someone's thoughts incarnate. How special to have that in your hands, particularly when that someone is far away, or no longer around. Unfold that paper, and there they are talking to you once again. This is probably why I've saved all of my letters in a shoebox.

Or, to put it another way, think about people from history. Consider the allure of a book called *The Collected Letters of [Literally Anyone]*. What an intimate window into that person's mind. It truly makes the past come alive. Which makes me wonder, for those future people reading about us, will the "collected emails" have the same ring to it? Rhetorical question, obviously. I'd venture to guess this is why a handwritten letter still has so much power. And why it seems to be the most promising method of reaching someone who is still alive.

Fan mail has always been a thing, of course, but how many DMs is one written letter worth? 1,000? 10,000? The barrier to entry is so low. Maybe it's 100,000. However it shakes out, taking the time to sit down, write a letter, seal it, stamp it, put it in the mail . . . that will always mean something more.

I once sent a letter with a story I wrote to Yvon Chouinard, founder of Patagonia. I had worked at Patagonia while in college and the story was about rock climbing but, really, I just wanted an excuse to tell the man that I admired him. To my great surprise, he wrote back. Chouinard's encouragement to keep writing and climbing, literally and figuratively, has never lost its luster.

Speaking of fame, it's worth mentioning that a number of noteworthy people have worked for the postal service: William Faulkner, a true man of letters, the folksinger John Prine, Walt Disney, and even a pre-Dunder Mifflin Steve Carrell.

This talk of letters may all seem quaint and antiquated, but isn't that the point? The antithesis of email, the opposite of efficiency, the antidote to getting riled up when someone hasn't responded to your email within two hours. In other words, the things which make letters obsolete are also what makes them endearing. Multiple days to send, multiple days to reply . . . that kind of space relieves the pressure of our split-second digital communication.

Maybe it's no surprise that the last person to regularly send me letters was my grandmother. There were the usual suspects—birthday cards, holiday cards—but also completely random things: interesting newspaper clippings, minor holiday (i.e. Halloween) cards, or notes for no real reason at all.

Now that she's passed, they're pretty much all I have left of her voice—which means my mailbox is just full of bills, grocery coupons, and recurrent solicitations from the local HVAC guy who *really* wants to replace my furnace. That's a real waste.

The philosopher Bertrand Russell is said to have written over 100,000 letters in his life. (For those counting, that's five letters a day for 54 years.) I'm probably averaging three/year right now. I think we'd all do well, myself included, to sit down and write a letter to someone we care about, even to simply say "I care about you" and nothing else. I'll start with my mom.

Here's to bad handwriting and good relationships.

HOW TO LIFE HACK
A STORY ABOUT SLOWING DOWN

I'm sick of the promise of instant gratification. Hacks for everything, pills for everything, tricks for manifesting the good life without any effort at all. Snake oil salesmen have been around since the dawn of civilization, dressed up in whatever clothes the day requires for them to pawn their promises. But, as it's been since the beginning, none of this is real.

I was talking to a friend the other day about life hacks and he asked: "What if life hacks, in the end, make *you* a hack?" No one wants to be a hack. A hack job is a job poorly done. No matter how much we glorify hacks as workaround to success, nothing gets you there except the actual work. The grind, the hustle, the hours on end putting your head down and getting into it.

It's not our fault, exactly. We've been sold this bill of goods by hucksters capitalizing on the human inclination for results, and the chance to bring that goal sitting on the horizon a little closer. Yet somehow we're all surprised when things we've barely fought to acquire fail to deliver satisfaction. The instant gratification disappears nearly as fast as it arrives. As they say: easy come, easy go.

So what's the antidote? Long-term projects.

Commitment to something where the end lies beyond the horizon situates your mind in the practice itself: the practice of living, of creating, of growing. And, slowly, you might start deriving satisfaction from the practice and not the results, ironically making the actual results that much more attainable.

I'm no great example; however, some things in my life require this mindset. Building custom homes, for instance, often takes two years. We have our blueprints—the end goal conceptualized—but on the daily I show up and move the needle a fraction of an inch, one stud, wire, window at a time. The novel I'm trying to sell to a publisher took three-and-a-half years to write . . . one word at a time.

Perhaps more universal is physical fitness, which also captures the difficulty of pulling this off. My water polo coach in high school always said: it takes three weeks to build your fitness, three days to lose it. Because it's all about the practice. The effort must never stop. No coasting allowed (that's called dying). So don't stop. DON'T STOP!

The thing is most people stop. It's easier to crack a beer, turn on Netflix, and check out every night than gain what you actually want in life by these almost imperceptible increments. And these people wonder about those "overnight success" stories. Overnight success does not exist.

My favorite quote is often attributed to Goethe: "At the moment of commitment, the universe conspires to assist you." The universe knows when you're committed. All the trials and tribulations are merely tests of your commitment. Pass the test. Keep going. Even if the rest of the world ignores you, the universe sees you.

Few people want to hear the truth that there are no hacks in life. We're surrounded by glossy visions of the future, all just as disposable as the goods being pedaled to get us there. This kind of thinking is absolutely everywhere. Take the news, the endless scroll, the noise is deafening. Each rapid-fire segment, every new post is another bid to make us care, yet all it really does is lead to apathy, indifference.

I feel that indifference. To the news, to social media, to a lot of things. I feel it all the time. But we've got to be careful—indifference is the putrid smell of commitment rotting. And as we said, commitment is the key. So when indifference creeps in . . . kill it. Consume it. Convert it into the committed energy for something else.

Now sometimes there's only so much you can say about a thing before action must overtake words. So there it is. As Lao Tzu said: "A journey of a thousand miles begin with a single step."

Get walking.

HOW TO KILL YOUR EGO (IN THE WILD)

A STORY ABOUT STAYING HUMBLE

Here's a question: look out your window... what's the biggest thing you see?

For most of us, that's a building, or many buildings, maybe even a row of skyscrapers along the skyline. Such a view might lead one to believe humans are pretty special—and when the biggest thing in sight is manmade, that's a reasonable take. Which leads to another question: what does this do to our collective ego?

A decade ago I lived in Denver, sixteenth-floor apartment facing west, with a glorious view of downtown and the Rocky Mountains beyond. Every day I pushed that button in the elevator with a puffed up chest thinking I was pretty cool rising up to the top floor. In the end, I lasted one year.

The thing that ultimately drove me out wasn't the noise or crowds or anonymity, but the utter lack of anything wild—every park and waterway had long been reconceived from its natural state, razed and reconstructed by the hands of man—the realization that no matter how tall that gold dome of the capitol, it had nothing on the mountains towering over the city, twenty miles away.

When the biggest thing in sight isn't a building but a mountain, it changes your perspective. Both in scale and in time. The mountains couldn't care less what we do as people. The youngest mountain was here long before us; and the oldest now will remain long after we're gone. Take the Appalachian mountains, formed when Earth's landmass was still in Pangea—now the chain is half in North America and half in Europe.

Something like a mountain keeps us humble, keeps us small in the best kind of way. The same goes for oceans. (And though I want to say the same for forests and rivers, the clearing and damming of these wild spaces gives the false sense of human superiority.) Nevertheless, we can always use a reminder.

It's no wonder thousands of writers have referenced these grandest of natural places. Take John Muir: "Climb the mountains and get their good tidings. Nature's peace will flow into you as sunshine flows into trees. The winds will blow their own freshness into you, and the storms their energy, while cares will drop away from you like the leaves of Autumn."

Yes! And yet there's a fundamental problem with ideas like this. They place nature as the *other*, the something else, the place we don't live *here* but which exists *elsewhere*. This perspective is flawed because instead of seeing ourselves as part of nature at all times, it makes us exceptional.

But humans are not the exception to the rule of nature. For the past 12,000 years we have indeed been bending the environment to our will, when we started farming and domesticating livestock as opposed to hunting and gathering, otherwise known as the neolithic revolution. Of course, civilization as we know it would not be possible without this development, but it's worth noting that hunter-gatherers had more leisure time than we do now.

As Charles Eisenstein notes in his book *Sacred Economics*, even the biggest private estate pales in comparison to the territory of early humans. Wild animals have more freedom than we do.

Kind of puts a damper on hustle culture. Even with all our time-saving conveniences—household appliances, automobiles, the internet—we've built a society hellbent on working us into the ground. And for what? Corporate benefit packages?

Before getting into what might be done about it, I think it's worth outlining the bigger picture of the planet's history for some perspective. In the last 500 million years, Earth has seen five mass extinctions. Through each extinction event, life has carried on. When some species died out, others flourished. The asteroid that killed the dinosaurs, after all, made room for us—humans, mind you, have been around for merely 300,000 years.

Yet this still feels abstract, too big to comprehend, but like a fractal that repeats itself to an infinitesimally small scale, the same forces that led to these events are at play today.

We tend to overcomplicate things when it comes to our species' past, convincing ourselves that what happened to humans a hundred, a thousand, even ten-thousand years ago is not happening anymore, but you barely need to crack the history books to see the correlation between humans and the environment.

For instance, the latest theory of why people abandoned the great cliff dwellings of Mesa Verde in Southwest Colorado was that they simply ran out of firewood. And there are thousands of examples like this, most featuring people whom we assume were "in tune" with the environment simply because they were of an earlier time. With our modern separation from the natural world, and our blustery attitude toward dominance, this ignorance is only exacerbated.

The point is our actions have consequences. This is not news, of course. The message is subtle, however, and if there's one thing an ego cannot parse out it is subtlety.

A good friend of mine put a sticker on his snowboard: STARVE THE EGO, FEED THE SOUL. Considering the terrain required to use it, that is a perfect place for such a statement. As we said, the mountains keep us humble, and sliding down them is merely a form of marginally controlled chaos—which is about as good as it gets living on this planet, not only for fun but in our day-to-day life just as well. Because control is an illusion.

If we accept this, then perhaps our perspective can change. The wonders of nature are unfathomable; trying to control any of them is like trying to slay the hydra, whereby as soon as we meddle with one feature, two more appear that must be dealt with. So maybe we ought to lay off a bit, give nature a chance to do what she does best: support life.

I take solace knowing that so long as the sun shines, life will go on. The question is: will humans be a part of it?

This isn't really about the environment at all. It's about us. As an oddly-appropriate example, I once saw a sign above a water-free urinal which read, and I'll paraphrase here: By using this urinal you are helping the environment to conserve a whole lot of water every year. But we're not helping the environment, we're helping *ourselves*; we confuse conservation with an act of charity toward the planet, when it's actually an act of charity toward us.

If we kill the ego, we kill the selfishness that's gotten us here. The Stoic philosopher Epictetus once said: "Wealth consists not in having great possessions, but in having few wants." Perhaps that is the mantra we ought to adopt. Not seeking endless growth (looking at you GDP), but finding contentment in the beauty we already have here on Earth, living in accord with it, and finding humility in doing so.

And, lastly, a few practical notes: take more nature walks, know your farmer, and whatever you do, remember no matter how big we think we are, there's always a mountain out there bigger.

FOREST/MACHINE

A SHORT STORY

Machine kills the Forest,
Forest kills the Machine

THE UNDERRATED PLEASURE OF PAYING CASH

A STORY ABOUT $$$

The other week I came into a couple hundred bucks, cash. I don't typically have dollar bills in my wallet, but I'm old enough to remember when that was the norm—a handful of coins jangling around, actually handing someone a tip, even making change behind the register—so I've been spending the money, except when I can't because the place doesn't accept cash.

The other night I tried a new pasta place in town: walking in not to be greeted by a person but a screen on the wall. On the screen I placed my order, paid, tipped, and in a few minutes had the food delivered without so much as a pleasantry. And I had to ask myself, is this really what we're after?

It's no news that we basically have a cashless society. If we're not swiping plastic, it's scanning QR codes or tapping our phones. We take this sort of progress for granted—the inevitable evolution of a society obsessed with efficiency and convenience—but do we want an efficiency so complete that human connection itself becomes an inconvenience?

In spite of ourselves, I think the answer is no.

It's sort of become a project to prove this whilst spending my cash. Every time I hand it over, I feel like I'm putting the *action* back into the transaction and interaction, taking it from anonymous to personal. There's an actual exchange of goods and services. And it's way more satisfying to drop a few bucks in the tip jar than to select that box on the screen. In those extra few seconds when the cashier makes change, maybe we even have a little conversation.

Sidebar: studies have shown that the key to longevity is in our social connections, not just with friends and family, but in these passing conversations, too.

The rising anonymity in our financial transactions is predicated upon abstraction. For thousands of years money existed in the physical realm—first in the form of coinage and later fiat currency—now our cashless society has debased the value of these interactions, reducing them to figures in a digital ledger book, out of sight and out of mind.

The tangibility of cash mitigates the modern loss of personal connection. But it also helps us financially, too.

We've been conditioned inside this society to consume. Consumption feels good. Why else is it so satisfying to get that box in the mail? Or to finish the last of the orange juice and throw the carton away? We're taught that products are *meant* to be consumed: we receive the joy of that potential energy upon purchase and the pleasure of spending the kinetic energy upon use.

Good citizens, so we're told, need more, more, more. And a cashless society promotes that ideology more than one which uses tangible currency, exactly because cash is the more satisfying way to pay. You can literally feel it being spent. On the other hand, swiping plastic for a $10 and $1,000 charge take the same amount of effort, which both obscures the amount of money going out and reduces the satisfaction of consumption, thereby making us do it more. So although, as the phrase goes, the cash burns a hole in my pocket, I actually think I spend it more wisely than when I use my card.

It's almost as if with credit cards we don't get to enjoy the fruits of our labor, or what, in his book *Die With Zero,* Bill Perkins calls our "life energy." The idea that in its balance money captures all the effort we've expended to make it. When we lose the tangibility of money, it's all the more easy to forget the real-world implications of spending too much . . . that is, debt.

We're not to blame as individuals, exactly. This is a societal problem. To illustrate: as a sophomore at the University of Colorado I went into my advisor's office to inquire about taking a class on personal finance. She thought about it for a minute, this being a four-year federally-funded institution, and finally said, "I think you'll have to go to a community college for that." If that's not fucked up, I don't know what is. Financial literacy is non-existent in most of our educational system. And we wonder why people are so underwater.

So let's accept that the abstraction of money does not serve the individual: not from a financial perspective, and not in the way of personal connection. The solution? We must be intentional with how we spend it, in both form and in function.

For instance, don't let convenience replace interpersonal communication (e.g. hey DoorDash, drop the food off at my front door, no contact) and instead let it foster connection. And also be sure to situate money in the larger context of our society.

In the end, of course, money is merely a tool. Take it from this homebuilder that tools are best used in your hands. So hit up the ATM, cash out a few twenties, and have a nice little conversation with the next cashier you see.

BUILD YOURSELF LIKE A HOME
A STORY ABOUT CONSTRUCTION

As I've said, I make my living as a custom homebuilder. That phrase, *making a living*, seems appropriate when you consider how much time we spend working—but, more importantly, how our work shapes the way we see life. So, I'll run through a few things that building houses has taught me about building a life.

Let's start with the construction itself.

#1 SURVEY: The first step of every home means staking claim on some plot of earth. For a new house that means buying a piece of property; but as individuals we have no choice where we're originally built—can't pick your parents—same goes for much of this early construction, but we'll get to that.

#2 EXCAVATION: Shovels in the ground. This is about embedding into the earth. For a house, of course, that means staying put; for us, I believe the most important part of building a life isn't in the actual construction at all, but tapping into something greater than ourselves and staying humble, the basis for all the work to come.

#3 FOUNDATION: Now the building begins. If the foundation is flawed, everything else is compromised. What's a personal foundation? Our sense of self: self-worth, self-love, desire, values. Our whole life bears on this. And if it's weak, well, I'd find it hard to trust that structure.

#4 FRAMING: The bones of the house. The body. Strong timbers require good nutrients, as do healthy bodies. We must nourish ourselves, because everything else is affixed to the framing.

#5 ELECTRICAL / PLUMBING / HVAC: We have the wires, the pipes, the ducts, analogous to our various internal systems. I think of it as the importance of fresh air, clean water, ample energy, the lifeforce.

#6 FINISHES: Finally, there are the finishes. What other people invariably notice first, the superficial beauty which obscures all that lies beneath, the façade. As the cliché goes, it's the beauty on the inside that matters, and these finishes ultimately mean little—they'll get remodeled, eventually. Let me tell you: if you don't already have it within, fancy tile will not bring you happiness.

Before this metaphor gets tiresome, though, let's get away from this idea of new construction because that's not what we're working with here. We're hardly agents in the personal home given to us by our parents. They build much of it for us: in the way they raise us, the situations and circumstances in which we're placed, the expectations and prejudices we're exposed to. This is the structure we're handed when we gain our own consciousness. For those of us with kids, it's something with which we must take great care in remembering.

Gaining independence, then, has little to do with leaving the actual family home and everything to do with realizing you are the sole owner of the personal home you've been given. Subsequently, this often requires some renovation.

For one, the home we're handed doesn't always suit our taste. And two, times change. Design is an evolutionary process. What was once in style is out, our tastes evolve, what we then wanted, we no longer desire . . . so we remodel.

I received a beautiful take on this in conversation recently, when someone told me they were tearing their life down to the studs so they could rebuild. That's what we have to do sometimes, isn't it?

You roll up your sleeves, grab the sledgehammer, get into some fucking demolition. And once the space is emptied, the dust settled, a vision of what and how to rebuild becomes clear. Design never ends. It continues in real time, an evolutionary process of decision-making that can only be understood as each prior phase falls into place.

But that's where this metaphor ends, because we are dynamic creatures, not stuck in place like a house. We move, we shift, we see new places every day. And we carry that sense of home within us. Yet we all know there's a difference between a house and home.

There is a feeling when you walk into a home, a true home, which can only be described as comfort. You feel this sense of comfort, too, when you meet certain people. This is when you know someone has built a real home inside themselves. The question we must ask ourselves is whether the home inside of us now is the home in which we'd actually like to live?

In the end, homebuilder is not the right name for what I do. I build houses. Building a home is a personal affair. I'm still working on it myself.

TAKING PUNCHES
A SHORT STORY

Saturday evening I was flipping through the channels and came across an old boxing match. One of those classic reruns: the 1982 Heavyweight championship, Tex Cobb vs Larry Holmes. Sick of the news, I cracked another beer, adjusted my back pillow and settled into the recliner.

Dolores made a good lasagna that night. The house still smelled like ground beef and tomato paste. I always said she must be part Italian. That had become our joke—my Dolores is as Irish as a Kennedy.

She yelled in from the kitchen. "Hal, what are you doing in there?"

The crowd cheered and cheered as Howard Cosell introduced the fighters.

I wouldn't have thought it from looking at him but Tex had never been knocked off his feet. The big man strutted around his corner with a nose hammered down like a 16-penny nail. I thought: hell, any man who can take a beating and stay on his feet earns my respect.

We get ready for first-round action! Cosell squawked. The bell rung and Cobb came out swinging like a barroom brawler. Holmes ducked, laying a combination across Cobb's sideburns. The crowd roared.

Dolores came into the doorway, wiping her hands on her apron. "Hal, can we talk?"

Every night she wanted to talk. She sat down at the walnut desk in the corner of the room and untied the apron, folding it neatly like some kind of satin blouse.

"Will you speak with someone at school tomorrow?" she asked.

"Tomorrow is Sunday."

"I don't have money to buy groceries."

"Put it on the card," I said, taking a drink.

A class professional versus a club fighter, said Cosell.

"I'm worried." Dolores picked at her fingertips. "If you'd only try talking to them again."

"They gave me their answer."

"Please, Hal. Won't you just—"

"Jesus H. Christ, Dolores." I twisted around and pain shot through my back. "I've already asked them a thousand ways."

Despite his number of KOs, Tex is an arm-puncher. There's not a lot of crispness to his punches.

Dolores ran her hands over the greys in her hair. "So, you've given up then."

"I have *not* given up."

"Then what would you call it?"

"Thirty-five years of my life!" I swallowed the rest of my beer and jammed the can in beside the cushion. "Don't act like I had a choice in it."

"Hal, all I am saying is—"

"Listen. I can't change their minds. I'm a shop teacher. No high school *wants* shop class anymore."

Blood from the nose of Randy "Tex" Cobb! Cosell declared.

I lowered my voice. "Things have changed, okay? Kids don't care about the trades. Learning how to accurately use a miter saw, that's for gorillas."

Larry counter-punching beautifully.

Dolores's lips tightened. She hadn't seen what I had. She hadn't been hammered by these young parents. Like when Ricky Tallet's mother got up at parent-teacher night and yelled in front of everyone: "I want my boy to get into college! He needs to be learning computer science, not carpentry. This is the 21st century!"

It made me sick. Never mind Ricky Tallet was a fine woodworker, a real talent. I'll never forget the smile on his face when he finished his wall clock project. The pride he'd gotten from it . . . what a waste.

Cobb's arms hung on the ropes between rounds. *His head must have been carved out of Mount Rushmore, and he certainly has a granite chin, but is this a palatable match? You decide.*

"Can we just talk about how we're going to pay our bills this month?" Dolores tapped the walnut desk in front of her.

That desk.

We weren't even married when I'd built it apprenticing for Arthur Jacques. I remembered it like yesterday hauling that thing into to our first apartment. Took up half the living room. We'd laughed about that for a long time.

"Let's sell the desk," I suggested, knowing what it would do.

"Hal!" Dolores spread her hand on the lacquered wood like I was going to wrestle it out to the truck right there. "This desk means so much." Wrinkles spread down my Dolores's cheeks.

Look at how swollen the poor man's face is. There's no sense in letting him stay, hoping he'll get a lucky punch in, because it isn't worth the price.

"We just need to make ends meet until we figure this out," she said. "You'll find work again. I know it."

"How?" I hooked my thumb on my collar. "I've been working my whole life. All I have to show for it is this bad back. I'm not a young man, anymore."

Dolores picked her fingers again and started to say something. She cut herself short.

"What?" I asked.

"No. It's foolish."

"Tell me."

"Well—" Tears crept into Dolores's eyes. "Maybe you could ask someone for a loan."

All of my friends were retiring and for the first time in my life I couldn't put food on the table. I hadn't made that many mistakes. I stared at my lap. What the hell happened?

Dolores was crying now. "I'm sorry."

Lord knows, maybe this man can stand up and take it for 15 rounds. What does that prove? Who knows what the after effects will be.

I swallowed hard. I'd never meant to hurt her like this.

"Dolores . . ." I pushed off my chair and shuffled toward her. Then I unlocked the bottom desk drawer, removing a creased envelope.

Dolores wiped her eyes. "What is this?"

I stared at the ceiling tiles, watching the lines between them disappear into the wall corners. "I haven't been honest with you."

Dolores's lips parted as she opened the envelope. "I don't understand."

"After my back went, these checks started coming. But when I got the first—" I scratched the stubble on my jaw. "Ah, hell, Dolores. You know I'm not one of those people."

Dolores took my hand into hers, her skin too rough for such a good woman.

I glanced at the television. Cobb was still on his feet. Only the muffled sound of him taking punches broke the silence in the room. He wouldn't go down.

He just wouldn't go down.

WHO ASKED FOR THIS?

A STORY ABOUT CHOICES

When his friend wrote a letter asking for some life advice, a twenty-two-year-old Hunter S. Thompson replied that if you don't deliberately choose the circumstances of your life, the circumstances will soon choose your life for you.

Whenever I need a reminder to own my life's choices, I revisit this letter—and it's worth reading the whole thing—though lately I've been thinking this sort of examination might be relevant well beyond myself. For, what applies to one individual often applies to them en masse, to a whole society, to a whole country. As Socrates said: "The unexamined life is not worth living." I guess I'd add that, perhaps, an unexamined culture is not one worth living in.

THE STATE OF AMERICAN CULTURE

When I started in construction all the guys would take lunch together, sitting on buckets, shooting the shit, getting to know each other; now, for the most part, everyone sits on the same buckets and stares at their phones.

In my mind, that captures our culture in a couple of ways: one, a lack of community, and two, our ever-present state of distraction.

I'm guilty as anyone, but I didn't ask to kill time scrolling on my phone. The thing just seemed to appear in my hand, as it did in everyone's, and the next thing I know my free time just sheds away. Now, *I* might not have asked for it, but *someone* did.

Every cultural moment, for better or worse, is a product of the commitment of a few and the indifference of many. In a society distracted by convenience, it seems all the easier for those few to get their way.

What's our current culture in America? The writer Ted Gioia says our culture has flattened and homogenized in the name of corporate profit. I'd argue so has our humanity.

At one point in the not so distant past landing Neil Armstrong and Buzz Aldrin on the moon brought Americans together in triumph. The last time we all came together as Americans might have been 9/11. I was only 15 at the time, so I can't be sure, but it felt that way.

What's a recent cultural event in America that brought people together? Setting aside increasingly epic natural disasters, one that comes to mind was the local opening of a Buc-ee's super gas station, which saw people lined up for miles for the chance to try fifty different flavors of beef jerky, watch choreographed barbecue chopping, and buy some Buc-ee's branded merchandise—which incidentally reminds me of the time In-N-Out Burger opened a few years earlier, for which people apparently waited in a fourteen-hour-long drive-thru.

I think Gioia is right to call out the corporatization of our culture. Couple that with the apathy of most people, if not outright enthusiasm for this, and it feels like we are literally consuming ourselves.

A SOCIETY OF CANNIBALS

The Ouroboros is an ancient symbol of a snake with its tail in its mouth. A common meaning is that of infinity or wholeness, but these days I see it as the mascot of a society which has cannibalized itself. Or, more particularly, one part of society intentionally eating another, without realizing the consequences.

Which reminds me of the time I worked on a cattle ranch that had been in continuous operation since the 1870s and some school kids came out to learn about it. At one point we stopped at the slaughterhouse, a small shed with some hooks on the ceiling, and one student earnestly asked: "Wait, you have to kill the cow to get a steak from it?" This kid has grown up and now manages a private equity firm.

Community cannot be commodified. Trying to squeeze everything in life for maximum profit, justified in the name of convenience and efficiency, kills our communities and our culture. Because community takes time to build. Ironically, a strong community likely leads to the best long-term profit but apparently that's not something quantifiable in our instant-gratification lifestyle. I'm no economist but we seem to have consumed our way to the bottom, through the bottom even, creating an ulcer through our communities where we as individuals have fallen, alone and lonely.

This is not a coincidence. Consider Facebook's original motto: move fast and break things. It turns out that's exactly what's happening, and the "stuff" being broken is our community, our mental health, our environment.

I can see how all of this sounds pretty pessimistic, and honestly sometimes I wonder if it wouldn't be best to hit rock bottom so we can see it all clearly, but I'm not without hope.

I MEAN, WE HAVE A PROBLEM, RIGHT?

Convenience creates complacency. Interestingly, *convenience* and *conventional* share the same root word, the Latin *convenire*, meaning "to agree." Perhaps we ought to start being more unconventional?

I had a college professor who said literacy today is not the ability to read and write, but the ability to understand the bias behind the messages we receive: in other words, what people are trying to get us to do. By that measure, we are fairly illiterate. The technologists have their agenda—it's posted on every door—but we can't read, so it comes as a real shocker when we get evicted from a life we understand into their vision of the future. (AI, anyone?)

Then again, we're a society that refuses to use reusable bags at the grocery store, even though we know how bad plastic bags are for the environment, but the convenience is just too great to overcome. At this point, only ignorance or laziness explains such action.

The point is good things are often inconvenient, and well worth it. The things we take for granted, the things we consider conventional, they're not neutral or unbiased occurrences. They serve someone's interests.

When you don't know how you got someplace, it seems inevitable, unchangeable, easy to take for granted as the new status quo, and we move forward as if there's nothing we can do to change it. But of course we can change it—all we need to do is pay attention.

Paying attention is the difference between driving the car, sitting in the passenger seat, and being blindfolded in the trunk. Many of us are tied up and don't even know it.

SO . . . STAY CURIOUS

At the close of that letter I mentioned at the outset of this piece, Hunter S. Thompson explains that we don't have to do something for our entire lives if we'd rather not. But if we decide against changing anything, might as well convince ourselves we had no choice.

That sounds pretty miserable. And I'm pretty sure there's only one way to avoid it . . . owning our present circumstances, then changing them accordingly.

I try to own my problems. It often sucks. But it's better than playing the victim. We, America, need to own our problems and stop shirking responsibility. Not blame them on other people: People that don't look like us or think like us or love like us. Our country's problems aren't the fault of the undocumented immigrant down the street or the trans kid at school. It's not even Mark Zuckerberg's or Elon Musk's fault. No, it's your fault. It's my fault. It's *our* fault.

The Navy SEAL Jocko Willink calls this "extreme ownership." Sometimes I willingly choose to mindlessly scroll on my phone. Sure, it's in the technologists interests that I do so, but they are not compelling me to do it. And the same can be said for so many of our collective problems.

We got here through a lack of vigilance.

So, who asked for this? We did. We asked for every bit of it. And we deserve it all. But, we can decide to be aware of what we're asking for, change the ask, and then we'll deserve that too.

WE'RE OUT OF CONTROL

A STORY ABOUT LETTING GO

Surprising exactly no one, I was voted "most laid back" in high school. I also heard from almost every teacher that I was "not fulfilling my potential as a student." While at the time these seemed like unrelated items in an otherwise unremarkable path to graduation, turns out they are exactly the same thing.

Our nature, obviously, cannot be changed: being born laid-back or uptight, left-brained, right-brained, black or white. These things are out of our hands—how we use these fixed traits, though, is the key.

Coasting through high school, I had embraced going with the flow, wearing that laissez-faire attitude like some lazy badge of honor. However, when it came time to make something of myself, post-graduation, it suddenly felt like a curse, like I was a person born without conviction. And it took flailing around for the better part of a decade to realize the truth that I'd rather observe what's going on around me than intervene, not from avoidance but more a curiosity of how things will play out without my influence. The trick, I eventually understood, was in learning how to embrace my nature and put it to good use.

I've come to learn many writers are like this. In *The Electric Kool-Aid Acid Test*, Tom Wolfe immortally detailed the late '60s scene, Ken Kesey and his Merry Pranksters, the Grateful Dead, and they say he was a fly on the wall, noting everything that happened without much input, producing, in turn, an unrivaled assay of the times.

Perhaps to you go-getters, this seems like a passive way to approach the world, even if it occasionally churns out literary gems, but I'd argue it's an *intentional* passivity, purpose-driven in its own right. Because pulled off successfully, it requires keeping one hand on the wheel with a clear direction in mind.

If that makes it sound like I've got things figured out now, I don't—but I've certainly gotten a better handle on where I want to go. Which raises an entirely different question: how much control over our lives do we even have?

The older I get, the more I see that control is an illusion, a fallacy, a fantasy, an imaginary plaything. It's not real. To prove it, pay attention to how many people remain utterly desperate for control: the manager making you come in on a Saturday to crunch out a few more TPS reports, flexing just because they can. Or maybe it's the lady accosting a birdwatcher in the park because he doesn't "look like he belongs." When people realize they can't control their own lives, they try to control everyone else's.

The desperation is so strong that people grab for every bit of control until the sand has slipped through their clenched fingers, but this—*this*—is the moment everything can change.

The Roman emperor Marcus Aurelius wrote: "You have power over your mind—not outside events. Realize this, and you will find strength." In other words, you don't control what happens, you only control how you respond.

As for controlling my response to outside events, I have one goal—no regrets. This isn't about limiting FOMO or living life to the fullest, it's not even about picking a path of purpose. No, this is about taking life as it comes; understanding that both the good things and the bad things had to happen to get you here. Change one thing and it would all be different. So when it's good, you must be grateful for all of it. And when it's bad—well, like George Harrison said, all things must pass—so it'll eventually get good again. Then it's back to gratitude for the long and winding road. No regrets.

Radical acceptance of everything that happens—that's probably the most hardcore thing anyone could do. Once false hope for control is purged out of your system, you might realize there was nothing there to begin with, nothing you really had control over beyond your own mind. And then, finally, you are free.

So here's to fighting like hell for what you can control and letting the rest happen as it will.

COLOR THE WORLD
A PARTING POEM

What really happens when the idealism fades?

The roots might stagnate but they don't go away.

When it slips from the branches, the wind blows them bare.

The leaves may lay different but they still lay somewhere.

While this tree of thought might wither and curl

Its children have ventured off

To color the world.

ACKNOWLEDGMENTS

To my people. You know who you are. Much love.

AUTHOR BIO

In my hometown, good kids become insurance salesmen. I did not. At eighteen I moved west to the mountains of Colorado. Sold clothes, raised cattle, financed real estate investors. Lived in the city. Lived in the country. Slept under the stars. On couches. In basements. Climbed rocks, wrecked cars, brewed beer. Loved women. Almost loved women. Hitchhiked, bushwhacked, bivouacked. Sat at backcountry campfires. Drank at backcountry bars. Married. Had a son. Had another. Built a home. Got divorced. Staying curious. And, still, I've wasted most of my time on the internet.

LEAVE A REVIEW

If you enjoyed any part of this book, do me a favor and leave a review. It matters more than you know.